Winning in the New York Small Claims Courts

A Simple, Step-by-Step Guide for Everyone

Tip the Scales of Justice in Your Favor sm

By Richard A. Solomon, Esq.

Winning in the New York Small Claims Courts
A Simple Step-by-Step Guide for Everyone

Published by:
> Rescue Media, Inc.
> P.O. Box 604173 Bay Terrace Station
> Bayside, New York 11360-4173

For information on how to purchase copies of this book
please visit:

www.smallclaimsbook.com

or call toll free 1-800-247-6553

Winning in the New York Small Claims Courts

Copyright 2002
First Printing 2002
Printed in the United States of America

Publisher's Cataloguing-in-Publication
(*Provided by Quality Books, Inc.*)

Solomon, Richard A.
    Winning in the New York small claims courts : a simple step-by-step guide for everyone / Richard A. Solomon. - - 1st ed.
    p. cm.
    Includes bibliographical references and index.
    LCCN: 2002091117
    ISBN: 0-9717965-0-5

    1. Small claims courts- -New York (State)- -Popular works. I. Title.

KFN5976.Z9S65 2002   347.747'04
                            QBI02-200352

This book provides information and general advice about the law. Please note that laws and procedures change frequently, and they can be interpreted differently by different people including lawyers and judges. Even appellate courts disagree with each other at times. For specific advice targeted to your specific situation, consult an attorney. No book, software, or other published material is a substitute for the interactive advice from a knowledgeable lawyer licensed to practice law in your state.

This book is sold with the understanding that the publisher is not engaged in rendering legal, accounting, or other professional service. Please check all telephone numbers, forms, and fee amounts charged by the Court as this information is constantly changing. One excellent internet reference is the official New York State Courts Website: www.courts.state.ny.us

This book is dedicated to Rea and Sol, whose love and support have made everything possible. Like their ancestors, they have enjoyed the freedom and personal growth allowed in the small business environment.

This book is also dedicated to Paul Solomon, the greatest brother anyone could ever have.

In the aftermath of the September 11, 2001 attack on the United States, I dedicate this book to my fellow New Yorkers who will survive and overcome the external threats to our freedoms and ideals. We will endure!

Can I really do this myself?   Yes–here's one testimonial

Dear Rich,

Thank you for encouraging me to submit a claim in small claims court against one of my vendors. I was quite satisfied and surprised how quick and easy it was. The cost for a business claim in New York City was $24.28 * and the Court date was assigned within six weeks. I did it all myself! I brought in my evidence on my appointed date and won the claim.

Enrica S.
Astoria, Queens

* this claim was filed before the July 2002 Postage Rate Increase. The current fee for a commercial claim is $24.79 to sue one defendant, plus $4.79 for each additional defendant (if any).

Definitions from the
Guide to Small Claims in District Court of Nassau County

adjournment--postponement of a case to another date

calendar--list of cases to be heard by the judge on a particular day

cause of action--claim by one person against another

claimant--person or company bringing a claim; also known as the plaintiff

counterclaim--claim by defendant against plaintiff seeking damages

CPLR--Civil Practice Law and Rules, the New York rules of procedure

cross-examination--asking questions of opposing party and their witnesses

damages--the amount of money a party seeks to recover in a lawsuit

defendant--person or business who is sued

execution--legal document authorizing Sheriff to seize personal property of a judgment debtor

inquest--hearing before a judge of a party's proof of claim where his opponent has failed to appear

judgment--legal document setting forth the outcome of a lawsuit judgment debtor--person against whom a judgment has been obtained. In general, someone who has not fully paid the amount due to a judgment creditor (one who has obtained a judgment)

lawsuit--process by which one person sues another in a court - the words "action" and "suit" have the same meaning as lawsuit

party--either plaintiff or defendant

plaintiff--person who sues another; also known as the claimant

subpoena--legal document commanding a witness to come to court to testify

summons--legal document when served upon a defendant begins a lawsuit

testimony--statements made under oath in a court by a party or a witness

witness–person who testifies in court on behalf of plaintiff or defendant

THIS BOOK:

1. Provides an easy to understand explanation of the rules and procedures of the New York Small Claims Courts.

2. Provides samples of the frequently used forms used in the small claims litigation process.

3. Will surprise you. Did you know that under section 332 of the New York State Vehicle and Traffic law, the Commissioner of Motor Vehicles is authorized to suspend the driver's license or registration of any person or company who fails to pay a judgment of more than $1,000.00 arising from the use or operation of any motor vehicle?

4. Is a resource guide because it answers questions such as "Where do I find a Sheriff?" and "How do I collect my money once I have won my case?"

5. Includes certain important laws with an easy to understand explanation.

6. Empowers the reader to bring or defend a small claims lawsuit with confidence.

7. Contains case studies from small claims court cases.

8. Contains practice tips that will help you save time and money.

9. Spares the reader from making mistakes by revealing information that is sometimes not documented within the Court rules.

10. Provides all the tools you need to be your own effective advocate.

Table of Contents

Getting Started

Chapter 1   The New York City Small Claims Courts

**Chapter 2   Some of the Other Small Claims Courts in
              the New York Metro area outside of New
              York City**

Chapter 3 Strategies for All Cases in Every County of New York State

Forms Index

11	Nassau County Small Claims Court Non-Commercial Claim Complaint Form
12	Nassau County Small Claims Court Commercial Claim Complaint Form
13	Suffolk County Small Claims Court Complaint Form
14	Suffolk County Commercial Claims Summons
15	City Court of White Plains Application Form (for a complaint)
16	City Court of White Plains Summons
17	City Court of White Plains Notice to Plaintiff
18	Affidavit of Service. (Blank, for use in all courts)
19	N.Y.C. Small Claims Court Affidavit is Support of Order to Show Cause to Vacate a Judgment and to Restore to the Calendar (can be modified for use in other courts.)
20	Order to Show Cause to Vacate a Judgment and to Restore to the Calendar, N.Y.C. Small Claims Court
21	N.Y.C. Small Claims Court Form 60, Information Subpoena and Restraining Notice

Getting Started

At some point, every person ponders the question of whether to enforce their rights as a creditor. All too often business owners do not pursue their rights because many claims are relatively small, and attorney fees are generally cost prohibitive. Others who wish to represent themselves are somewhat intimidated by the numerous rules and regulations associated with the Court system.

This book will provide you with the tools necessary to analyze your claim, choose the correct Court location, file a small claims case, sue the properly identified defendant, and either settle the case or go to trial. This book is also written for the defendant who has been sued and needs to quickly learn the process of defending oneself in a small claims situation. Whether you are the person bringing or defending the claim, the knowledge contained in this book will give you the confidence to enforce your rights in a Court of Law.

Throughout the book, I explain the jargon associated with the Court system and show you how to avoid wasting your valuable time in all stages of the collection process. My overriding goal for claimants reading this book is to help you avoid future litigation by teaching you how to limit your lending or credit risk. An ounce of prevention is worth more than a pound of cure and you will see how this is true in later sections of this book.

The most essential and possibly the most difficult part of the collection process for the claimant is collecting the money awarded by the Court to you in the form of a judgment. (A judgment is a Court created document detailing the outcome of a lawsuit.) This book will provide useful tactics and strategy on this difficult topic. Of all the topics I have taught on debt collection, this is the topic that generates the most questions from audiences.

How to use this book: start by browsing through Chapters One and Two to see where you should file your case. Determine which rules apply to your case and which forms you will need to fill out for that particular court. You may wish to read chapters one and two in their entirety to learn the common themes of the Statewide Small Claims Court system but it is not necessary. Pay particular attention to sections three and four of Chapter One to learn the techniques in filling out the forms with respect to the identity of the defendant, time limitations on suing, and interest rate calculation.

Your next step is to proceed to Chapter Three to begin your small claims court legal education. This is where you will begin to learn how to present your case in a simple but effective way while avoiding the traps of the Court system. You will be given a step-by-step approach so you will feel confident representing yourself. If you are the party bringing the case, you will learn how to select your evidence and witnesses, have the competitive edge in settlement negotiations, and if successful at trial, obtain a judgment and enforce it, which means collecting the money owed to you or your business. You will find all the information and reference material that you need from a model settlement agreement to the address and phone numbers of all the sheriffs in New York State. If you are a defendant, you will learn how to defend your case, determine whether you will need an attorney, and limit your risks as much as possible.

One final suggestion: if you have the time, visit the small claims court where your case will be heard and watch cases being processed. You will learn a great deal from simple observation especially after you have read this book.

Chapter 1
The New York City Small Claims Courts

Section 1   Introduction to the New York City Courts

The New York City Small Claims Courts allow you to bring a claim without the need for an attorney *if* your claim is for **three thousand dollars or less**. This book provides much more information than what appears in the free literature provided by the New York State Unified Court System, because it is based upon the experience of many years of small claims court litigation on behalf of clients, and on my own behalf.

NYC Small Claims Court locations as of the date of this publication: Check to make sure these addresses are still current

General Phone Number for all of NYC is 212-791-6000

New York County (Manhattan)
111 Centre Street
New York, New York 10013
212-791-6900 General Information. [Also 646-386-4500 or 3000]
212-374-8175 Supervising Clerk of the Small Claims Court
212-374-5776,79 Small Claims Clerk's Office

Bronx
851 Grand Concourse (Basement)
Bronx, New York 10451
718-590-3601 General Information
212-374-8082 Administrative Judge's Telephone Number
718-590-2693 Supervising Clerk of the Small Claims Court

Brooklyn (Kings County)
141 Livingston Street Room 201
Brooklyn, New York 11201
718-643-5069 General Information
718-643-7914 Small Claims Clerk's Office [also 718-643-7913]

Queens
89-17 Sutphin Blvd.
Jamaica, New York 11435
718-262-7100 General Information
718-262-7123 Small Claims Clerk's Office [also 718-262-7135]

Richmond County (Staten Island)
927 Castleton Avenue
West New Brighton, Staten Island, New York 10310
718-390-5417 General Information

Additional Resource Reference: www.courts.state.ny.us

The current limit on a Small Claims Court action is **THREE THOUSAND DOLLARS**. If your claim is larger than $3,000.00, you must bring the action in the New York City Civil Court where the jurisdiction is up to $25,000.00. If your claim is significant, you should seriously consider hiring an attorney.

The following Notices Appear in the Clerk's Office in **Manhattan** and most of these rules apply to all cases filed in the five counties of New York City:

- Attention: The Small Claims cashier register closes at 4:30 p.m. sharp. All money transacted must be completed by 4:30 p.m. No Exceptions. It is not sufficient to be on line by 4:30 p.m. After 4:30 p.m. no transactions will be processed.

- Courtroom is 111 Centre Street Room 353 at 6:30 p.m. The Court date has been pre-set and cannot be changed by the Clerk. This information will also be printed on your receipt.

- This office opens at 9:00 a.m. and closes promptly at 5:00 p.m. No money or checks can be processed after 4:30 p.m. NO EXCEPTIONS. On Thursday evenings only, small claims office hours are 5:30 p.m. - 8:00 p.m.

- PLEASE NOTE the party you are suing must be in New York City.

- If you represent a corporation, partnership or association, you must fill out a commercial claim form. Ask the Clerk for "form 70." Do not wait in line for this form. Filing fee $24.79 exact change. (Each additional defendant requires a separate "Form 70" and $4.79 more.)

- There is one line only. Please do not crowd the counter.

- Note: If you are a claimant over 65 years of age, disabled, or work at night, you are eligible to have your case heard in the daytime. Information about daytime sessions is available from the Clerk.

- If you are experiencing a problem that cannot be resolved by the employee assisting you, please ask for the assistance of the small claims supervisor, Ms. Ferrer x 5779.

- Please have your form completed and be prepared to proceed with your transaction when you reach the counter.

- Method of Payment: cash (exact change), money order, certified check

- Information booklet distributed upon payment of filing fee.

- The Civil Calendar Clerk is located in room 118.

- Zip Code Information, call 967-8585.

Resources near the Manhattan Small Claims Court Downtown Location

Photocopies:

Kinko's Copy Center
105 Duane Street (between Broadway and Church Streets)
212-406-1220

Post Offices:

Chinatown, 6 Doyer
212-267-3510

Canal Street Post Office
350 Canal Street (at Church Street)
212-925-3378

Chapter 1
The New York City Small Claims Courts

Section 2 Introduction to The New York City Commercial Court

The commercial claims part of the New York City Small Claims Court is limited to **business** related claims brought by a business. For example, the commercial part does not include cases where you have lent a cousin $400.00 dollars to buy a new set of tires for his car and you have not been paid back in over a year. You may bring that action in small claims court, but that scenario is not business related, and therefore not discussed in this section. The form for that type of case is FORM 1 and is discussed extensively in Chapter 1 Section 4 of this book.

Getting Started with a Commercial Claim

In order to commence a commercial action in New York City, you must first go to the clerk's office and fill out a claim form (usually printed on yellow paper) on both sides. This form appears as FORM 2 in the appendix section of this book and is provided as a sample. You will need to obtain an original form from the Clerk of the Court in order to initiate your claim.

When you file your claim, make sure to ask the Clerk to give you a copy of the Court rules which are provided without charge to the public. For your convenience in Court, copies of the Rules are included in this book:

Appendix 1, A Guide for the Use of the Commercial Claims Part, New York State Unified Court System (nine pages);

Appendix 2, A Guide to Small Claims in District Court of Nassau County (twenty-three pages).

Chapter 1
The New York City Small Claims Courts

Section 3 Filling Out the **Commercial** Claim/Complaint Form
[Form 2]

The key to successful litigation starts with properly filling out the complaint form. This is the document that actually starts your case. When you submit this form and pay the fee, you will be assigned a trial date. Note: this section applies only to cases brought by a business.

I. Claimant's Information

This is your business name and address. Your business must reside inside New York State in order to bring an action in Small Claims Court. Businesses located outside New York State can bring their claims in the New York City Civil Court. Generally the Civil Courts are in the same buildings as the Small Claims Courts. The filing fee for a Civil Court case is $35.00. However, you must be represented by counsel if the claimant (the creditor) is a corporation. Information on the Civil Court appears in the last section of this book.

In the New York City Small Claims Court, the Clerk serves the complaint by certified mail so you do not need to be initially concerned about how the complaint is served.

II. Defendant's Information

This is where you need to make sure that you are listing the correct "legal name" of the company or individual you want to sue. To verify corporate names, you can access New York State

Corporation information without cost by going directly to the New York State Secretary of State's office via the internet at **www.dos.state.ny.us**   All too often, claimant's sue the "wrong name" and because there are no assets under that name, the defendant purposely defaults in the case. The default judgment that you obtain will be worthless and you will have to bring a new lawsuit using the correct name of the defendant if you want to collect your money.

Case study:

> Creditor conducted business with a company that called itself "ABC&Q, Inc." The client sued in small claims court, and asked my law firm to enforce the judgment which means using a Marshal or Sheriff to collect the money pursuant to a Court finding. (By the way, the use of a Sheriff or Marshal is not automatic.) When my office conducted a background check in preparation for the enforcement, the New York State Secretary of State reported that no corporation ever existed under that name. A copy of the official document from the State Government appears as FORM 3.

> Now that we were certain that we had the wrong name of the debtor, we had to find the real name of the company. That was a lot harder to do once the client decided to sue and probably tipped off the debtor that the lawsuit was forthcoming. As you can imagine, debtors provide

information at the beginning of any relationship, not at the bitter end where their goal is to frustrate you by raising as many hurdles to collection as possible. Through time and effort, the correct name of the debtor was determined and a new suit was brought. The lesson is to do your homework the moment you start doing business with anyone to whom you are extending credit. Who are they, ask to see their business certificate or incorporation papers. Ask for a down payment and see how their name is listed on the check or credit card. Always make copies of checks made out to your business and keep this information on file for future reference.

Your defendant must reside within the five boroughs of New York in order to bring a lawsuit in the New York City Small Claims Courts. In the Queens County Clerk's office, a sign prominently states "PLEASE NOTE CAREFULLY IF THE PERSON OR ENTITY YOU WISH TO SUE IS LOCATED OUTSIDE THE FIVE BOROUGHS YOU CANNOT SUE HERE."

III. Claim (All the Subheadings in this Section Appear on the Claim Form)

"Amount Claimed"

 This is the amount you are suing for also known as your demand for money damages. Do not inflate your claim as this will only annoy the judge (or arbitrator) and cause you to lose

credibility. You cannot recover for your time in Court as some people believe. There is no "pain and suffering" here since that legal remedy only applies to cases alleging physical injuries.

Practice Tip: Do not add interest to the amount owed <u>unless</u> it is specifically agreed to in a written contract and signed by the debtor. The upper limit of <u>contractual</u> interest is 16%. This can only be enforced if the defendant signs a contract agreeing to pay this amount of interest in the event of late payment. Otherwise, the Court will add statutory interest (the rate determined by New York's legislature) at the rate of 9% to the judgment if you win.

"Date of Occurrence or Transaction"

This is the date that the money became due to you. This is an important date because the Court measures this date against the Statute of Limitations–the time the legislature has determined that you must bring your case by or forever lose the ability to sue on that specific claim. In New York, the time to bring an action for breach of contract (six years from the breach) is covered by the New York Civil Practice Law and Rules (known as the "CPLR") section 213.

The date of the breach of contract is also important because if you win your case, the Court will award interest at the rate of 9% from the date of the breach (CPLR 5004).

"Briefly state your claim here (Include Identifying Number(s)-Receipt #, Claim #, Account #, Policy # Ticket #, License #)"

Be concise, but include the details supporting your claim. The more precise you are, the more credibility will be given to your claim.

Example 1: Plaintiff is a construction equipment rental company with offices located in Queens County. Defendant rented equipment from plaintiff who has a written contract with defendant. Plaintiff's invoice total $1,145.23. Defendant made no payments even though this amount was due from March 20, 2001.

Practice Tip: Always include the names of individuals you interacted with.

Example 1a: Plaintiff is a construction equipment rental company with offices located in Queens County. Defendant's President John Q. Smith signed a written rental equipment agreement. Plaintiff sent invoices totaling $1,145.23. Defendant made no payments even though this amount was due from March 20, 2001.

*   *   *

Other examples:

Example 2: Bounced check: number 2242 issued by [Bank's Name and Address] dated 3/26/02. Bank charge (which defendant is responsible as a matter of contract) is $30.00. Thus $318.26, the amount of the bounced check issued by Mr. [Check Bouncer] plus $30.00 is $348.26.

Many cases are brought because a debtor has bounced a check.

Example 3: Transport and pick up of road plates for construction project on 57th Street and Madison Avenue in Manhattan. Invoice no. 5461 dated

12/31/01 is past due. A demand letter was sent on March 1, 2002. No response. The contractual amount sought is $3,000.00.

These examples should give the impression that you only need to give a very brief explanation focusing on the amount due and how it became due to you.

The Reverse Side of the Form [Form 2]:

Certification (NYCCCA 1803-a) (the citation to the left is to the New York City Civil Court Act)

I hereby certify that no more than five (5) actions or proceedings (including the instant action or proceeding) pursuant to the commercial claims procedure have been initiated in the courts of this State during the present calendar month.

Signature of Claimant

Signature of Notary/Clerk/Judge

*This certification must be signed in front of the clerk when you file the claim and pay your fee. You can also have your signature notarized, but we recommend signing before the clerk of the small claims court. As the form states: The Commercial Claims Part will dismiss any case where this certification is not made.

In case you are wondering why there is a five case per month limit, it is because the Courts do not want collection agencies flooding the Court with their cases. This is the one forum where an aggrieved plaintiff can sue without an attorney and obtain fairly quick results at a low cost. Should private commercial interests take over, the system would not be able to process those cases in addition to the tens of thousands of claims filed by individuals and small business owners.

Commercial Claims Arising out of Consumer Transactions

The reverse side of the complaint form [FORM 2 side b] also contains an additional certification for a commercial claim arising out of a "consumer transaction." If you are not sure whether your transaction falls under this category, please consult an attorney or ask the Clerk.

Certification (NYCCA 1803-A)

I hereby certify that I have mailed a demand letter by ordinary first class mail to the party complained against, no less than ten (10) days and no more than one hundred eighty (180) days before I commenced this claim.

I hereby certify, based upon information and belief, that no more than five (5) actions or proceedings (including the instant action or proceeding) pursuant to the commercial claims procedure have been initiated in the courts of this State during the present calendar month.

Signature of Claimant   Signature of Notary/Clerk/Judge

Practice Tip: The New York City Courts do not provide a form called "demand letter." Generally it is a written demand for a specific amount of money past due. The Nassau County District Court provides a blank demand letter which appears in this book as FORM 6 and it could be adapted by you for use in your New York City Cases.

Recommendation: send a final demand letter to convey your intentions and to establish a clear written record. Many clients send these letters by certified mail return receipt requested in order to have absolute proof of delivery.

Chapter 1
The New York City Small Claims Court

Section 4 Non-Commercial Cases

THE COURT RULES APPEAR in Appendix 3, <u>A Guide to Small Claims Court: New York City, Nassau County, Suffolk County 2001-2002</u> (33 pages)

<u>Filling Out the NYC Small Claims Court Non-Commercial Claim/Complaint Form</u> [Form 1]

I. Claimant's Information

The person bringing the case is called the claimant. Other similar names are creditor and plaintiff. Fill out the name and address neatly. Since many people are reluctant to provide a home telephone number on a public document, write in a day time work phone number.

II. Defendant's Information

This is where accuracy is essential. Make sure you have the correct spelling of the defendant's name and a current address. Remember, the defendant must be a resident of New York City. As the form states:

> " The legal name will be required in order to obtain an enforceable judgment. If the Defendant is a business, its full and correct business name should be obtained from the Office of the County Clerk in the county in which the business is located. You must indicate the proper street address of the defendant. A Post Office Box is not acceptable."

III. Claim

Do not inflate the amount of your claim as this will destroy your credibility with the Court. Only sue for the amount of damages that you have sustained and can prove.

The date of occurrence refers to the date the debt became due. Many small claims cases arise from motor vehicle collisions.

The form asks: "Place of occurrence, if Auto Accident" so do not forget to fill in this blank.

The form states that "If the Claim is as a result of automobile accident, the Claim must be Owner against Owner." This means that the claimant and defendant(s) must be the owners of the vehicles involved in the collision.

Check off the primary reason for your claim, and sign the form and submit it to the clerk along with your payment.

> Practice Tip: Make sure that your claim is brought timely, that is, within the time allocated by the New York State Legislature to bring a case, known as the "Statute of Limitations." In general, you have six years to bring an action based on contract and three years to bring a case based on negligence. Car accident cases are considered to be "negligence" cases.

Please refer to the analysis in Chapter 1, Section 3 regarding the claims section of the commercial claim form since many elements discussed there apply here as well, especially the explanation regarding the statute of limitations.

Non-Commercial Court Fees

The Court Fee for non-commercial cases: ten dollars for cases up to one thousand dollars, and fifteen dollars for cases up to three thousand dollars.

If you are bringing a wage claim for under $300.00, the fee is $4.79.

Chapter 1
The New York City Small Claims Court

Section 5 The New York City Small Claims Court Clerk's Office
(All N.Y.C. Cases)

The Clerk's office is generally open from 9:00 a.m. to 4:30 p.m. (Never try to file a claim on or close to the end of the day. Claimants have been turned away at what they thought was 4:28 p.m. Better safe than sorry in this circumstance.) You will note a sign in the office that states "NO CLAIMS CAN BE PROCESSED AFTER 4:30 NO EXCEPTIONS." This rule is strictly enforced.

To avoid long waits, do not arrive at 9:00 a.m. unless you arrive early and establish your lead position on line. The best time to file your complaint is in the mid afternoon (e.g., 2:45 p.m.). In some counties, the Clerk's office is open on Thursday evenings from 5:30 p.m. until 8:00 p.m. for the filing of new cases only. Call the Court and determine when the Clerk's office will be open, given governmental budget cuts and staff shortages.

The Courts are closed on Holidays so make sure that the Court will be open on any day that you are not sure of, such as Veteran's day. One excellent day to file papers is the day after Thanksgiving. The worst day to go to the Court is at the beginning of the month and on Monday mornings.

In some of the Clerk's offices, you will be instructed to take a number and wait. There are no exceptions for a quick question or in the instance when you need to return to the window after you have already completed your transaction. Other offices such as Manhattan have the claimants queue up in one line. Sometimes the Manhattan line is very long so allow for sufficient waiting time.

The Clerk's office accepts cash (exact change), certified checks, money orders and attorney's checks. Under no circumstances will the Court accept a personal or business check. If you pay in cash, bring exact change. If you do not have cash in the correct amount, you may be turned away. In general there are no convenient change machines in the Courts and at best you can only obtain quarters.

Practice Tip: if you think you will be utilizing the Small Claims Court more than once, take an extra complaint form and keep it on file in your office. You can fill out the form ahead of time and bring it already completed the next time you go to Court.

The Clerk will issue a trial date once you submit the completed form with your payment. Each additional defendant generally requires an additional payment.

Internet Reference: **www.ci.nyc.ny.us/html/dca/smallclm.html**

Court Forms

There are many times when the Small Claims Court Clerk will not provide a claimant or defendant with a form other than the complaint form or the information booklet if you cannot provide the index number (a case tracking number) of an active lawsuit. For example, the Court is reluctant to provide the Restraining Notice form because that form is to be purchased in the private sector. If one clerk does not help you, wait a while and try again at a different time. If all else fails, ask someone in the Clerk's office who may be an attorney or an experienced litigant. The Clerks can provide useful tips.

Trial Date Selection

Most important fact to remember about the trial date: you have no say on what date you will be given. There is a sign up for each day that says "if you file your case today, your trial will be March 9." This is a take it or leave it proposition. You cannot ask for a different date. Your only choice is to file on a different day if the date offered is not convenient for your schedule.

Practice Tip: Call the Clerk's office and ask "What trial date are you assigning today?" If the date is not good for you, wait a day or two and call back. The Court schedules about three hundred cases a day. If you call and find out that the assigned date is May 15, and when you appear to file, you are told "May 16" it may be because the Court has processed the full amount of cases allocated for one day. You may want to ask how many more cases will be accepted before the next calendar day is scheduled.

Incidentally, the New York City Small Commercial Claims Courts are in session on Monday through Thursday evenings.

If the trial date you are given becomes a problem for you, the Clerk's office cannot do anything to change the date. The only way to seek a new date is at the "Calendar Call" (a personal appearance; think of it like a "roll call.") on the scheduled trial date. If you find yourself in such a situation, have a trusted friend appear on your behalf and explain why you could not appear. If you do not appear at all, the Court will dismiss your action. If that happens, your only remedy is to file the action again and pay another fee.

Sometimes, claimants write to the Court asking for adjournments. This is not recommended at all. The Court has so many cases that it is only equipped to process questions at the Calendar Call. (More on the Calendar Call below.)

The only form in this book that relates to adjournments appears as FORM 7, "<u>Affidavit of Self-Represented Person in Support of Application for Adjournment.</u>" This is **NOT** a small claim form and was taken from the Office of the Self-Represented in Manhattan Supreme Court. You may wish to fill out a modified version of this form and have a trusted friend hand it in at the Calendar call if you are concerned that your friend cannot effectively communicate with the Clerk during the Calendar call. Again, this is only a suggestion.

What does the Clerk give you?

You will receive a form [an example of this form is FORM 8] with a receipt (save this for tax and litigation purposes) that states all of the following:

> Name of the Court
> The Court's address
> Today's date (that is the filing date)
> The index number (very important–it identifies your case. It is what a license plate is to a motor vehicle)

and the following statements:

> ONLY THE JUDGE PRESIDING AT THE HEARING CAN GRANT AN ADJOURNMENT. THE CLERK CANNOT

GRANT ANY CHANGE IN THE SCHEDULE DATE OF TIME.

Instructions to Claimant

Hearing

You must be present, with any witness(es) and/or other proof of your claim, at the time and place indicated above.

If your claim is for property damage, in order to prove your claim you must produce, at the time of trial, either:

(1) An Expert Witness (for example, a Mechanic)
(2) A Paid Receipt (itemized, marked "Paid," and signed),or
(3) Two Estimates for services or repairs (itemized and signed)

Practice Tips:

These rules are strictly enforced. If you bring only one estimate, you will be instructed to return to Court with the proper evidence, that is <u>two estimates</u>. If the receipts do not include your name or are unsigned, you will have difficulties with the Court and your claim. If you need to bring an expert, make sure that the expert will be available on the trial date. Also, most experts expect to be compensated for their time waiting and testifying in Court. Work this out ahead of time so there is no misunderstandings especially if the witness has to wait in Court for two different days because of Calendar congestion or adjournments requested by your opponent.

The form continues:
Once service of the Notice of Claim is complete, you may request the Clerk to issue a Subpoena for Records and/or a Subpoena to Testify, to compel someone to appear. Such Subpoenas are issued by the Court without any fee, but will be required to pay a fee to the person on whom the subpoena is served. Your request for such a subpoena must be made of the Clerk before the date of the hearing.

Practice Tip: If you can avoid subpoenas do so. Whenever you lose control over any aspect of your case, you are at the peril of delays, increased time and expense, and possible "no shows." Have all your evidence and testimony ready before you file. Remember, you are entitled to ask your opponent essential questions under cross-examination if your adversary testifies in their own defense. A more detailed analysis of the subpoena rules are listed below.

If you have not received a copy of the booklet "A Guide to Small Claims" or "A Guide to Commercial Claims," request one.

Practice Tip: Many times the Clerk's office is out of stock of these items. Make sure to check whether the rules you are provided by the Court are the current rules. Copies of the Rules are also included in this book.

Judges and Arbitrators

The Judge can only hear a limited number of cases at each session of the Court. Most hearings are held before volunteer arbitrators who are attorneys with at least five years of experience and thoroughly knowledgeable in the law.

> **Practice Tip:** Make sure that the arbitrator is not acquainted with any of the parties.

The decision of a Judge is subject to appeal but no appeal of an Arbitrator's decision is permitted since there is no official court transcript of Hearings held before Arbitrators.

> **Practice Tip:** It is not worth appealing a decision from Small Claims Court. The time and expense do not justify the effort especially when most appeals of defense verdicts are not successful. Have good evidence, be prepared, give it your best shot and then move on to other projects.

Either party may choose to have the case heard **only** by the Judge, by responding **"by the Court,"** at the time of the calendar call. If you request your case "by the Court" it is quite possible that you will have to return for trial at another time.

Practice Tip: A defense delay tactic is to always ask for a trial before a Judge. In one instance several years ago in which a doctor sued a patient for non-payment in Manhattan, the defense asked for a Judge trial and had the case delayed five times. It was not worth it for the doctor to have made five separate visits to the Court (and a sixth to file the claim). Always seek prompt resolution of your case by obtaining a Hearing as quickly as possible.

Once the complaint form [FORM 1 or 2] is submitted, the Court system then creates its own form and this form is sent to the defendant(s) by certified mail. The time lag between your submission and first appearance at night ranges from five to ten weeks depending on calendar congestion.

The form [FORM 8] continues with a section called Instructions for Answering the Calendar Call, but that will be discussed in Chapter 1, Sections 6 and 7.

Special Rules for Senior Citizens, Litigants with Disabilities, and Night Workers

The following Notice is posted in the N.Y.C. Small Claims Court:

New York City Civil Court Act, section 1815, provides an option to a claimant who is a senior citizen, a disabled person or a person whose normal work schedule requires him/her to work during evening hours to choose to come to Small Claims Court for a hearing during the day rather than in the evening.

Should you qualify and choose at the time of commencement of the Small Claims Court action to have your hearing during the day rather than in the normal evening hours of the Small Claims Court Part, you must provide the Clerk with adequate documentation of your qualification. The following documentation will be sufficient:

1. Senior Citizen. A medicaid card (author's note: the writer probably meant medicare), driver's license or other proof of showing that the claimant is 65 years of age or older.

2. Disabled. A medical note from a doctor [in accordance with section (c) above, a medical note will not be required if the claimant is visibly disabled for example, a person who is blind or is confined to a wheelchair] indicating that the claimant is "disabled"as defined in Executive Law Section 292(2) which states:

the term "disability" means (a) physical, mental or medical impairment resulting from anatomical, physiological or neurological condition which prevents the exercise of a normal bodily function or is demonstrable by medically accepted clinical or laboratory diagnostic techniques or (b) a record of such an impairment or (c) a condition regarded by others as such an impairment.

3. Night worker- A note on employer's letterhead with a telephone number for verification purposes indicating that the claimant is employed in a capacity which requires work in the evening hours during which the Small Claims Part holds evening hours.

Citation: S.C. Handout 101 (Revised effective 9/9/95)

What does the Clerk mail to the defendant?

Each defendant receives a form sent by certified mail which states the following:

NOTICE OF CLAIM AND SUMMONS TO APPEAR

Notice to Defendant: This Notice of Claim and Summons to appear is the start of a lawsuit against you. It should not be ignored. Your default may have serious consequences. YOU MUST BRING THIS NOTICE WITH YOU EACH TIME YOU APPEAR IN COURT ON THIS CASE.

Notice of Claim:

The Claimant asks Judgment in this court of $ (amount typed in) together with interest and disbursements on the following claim: (Example: Action to recover monies arising out of nonpayment for services rendered. Date of occurrence: _____.

Summons to Appear:

This claim is scheduled for a Hearing to be held in the Courtroom: [Street Address] Room (room number typed in) _____, New York (zip code) on (day of the week) (Date and Year typed in) at __ p.m.

You or someone authorized to represent you must appear and present your defense at the Hearing. If you wish, you may retain the services of an attorney to represent you at your own expense.

If you fail to Appear, Judgment will be entered against you by default even though you may have a valid defense. Only the Judge presiding at the Hearing can grant an adjournment. The Clerk cannot grant any change in the scheduled date or time.

Practice tip: If you are sued it is a mistake to simply default. If you have a valid defense, go to Court and argue your case. Make the plaintiff prove his or her case since it is always the person bringing the case who has the burden of proving the case known in legal terms as the burden of proof .

If you are sued and you are in the wrong, go to Court and either arrange for a payment plan or try to settle the action for an amount that is reasonable under the circumstances.

Chapter 1
The New York City Small Claims Court

Section 6   The Calendar Call – What is Announced in the NYC Courts

The following statement is read by the Court Clerk at the beginning of the Calendar Call.

Good evening Ladies and Gentlemen

Because of the large number of cases on tonight's Calendar it would be impossible for the Judge to try all of the cases. Therefore in addition to the Judge, we have many arbitrators available to assist the Court and try these cases.

The arbitrators are Court appointed experienced attorneys who have volunteered their time to try small claims cases. Most cases are heard by arbitrators.

When the Calendar is called, please stand and repeat your name.

If both parties are present you will get an immediate trial tonight if both parties agree to have an arbitrator try the case. However, if you choose to have your case heard by the Judge say "Ready By the Court."

Keep in mind you may have to return to Court several times before your case can be reached for trial by a Judge. When your case is sent to an arbitrator, there is a card which you will be asked to sign. Your signature on this card will indicate that you understand that the arbitrator's award is final and binding on both sides and that there is no appeal. However, if your case is tried by the Judge, it is possible to appeal from a Judge's decision. Please note that an appeal may be expensive and time consuming.

If only the claimant is present, and the defendant doesn't appear this evening, the claimant will be sent to an arbitrator for an inquest. Even if the defendant does not appear, you must still prove your case at an inquest.

If only the defendant is present and the claimant doesn't appear, the case will be dismissed.

If you need an adjournment, for example, to add an additional party, to change the amount [claimed as damages], or to make a request because you are not prepared to proceed, repeat your name and say "Application."

When you hear your case called, please stand up and answer with your name in a loud clear voice.

A copy of this announcement, made at the beginning of the Calendar Call, is posted in the lobby of the Queens Civil Court building in Jamaica.

Chapter 1
The New York City Small Claims Court

Section 7   Answering the Calendar According to the Court's Instructions

This information is quoted from FORM 8 and is directed to everyone. These are the Court's own instructions on how to answer the calendar call.

INSTRUCTIONS FOR ANSWERING THE CALENDAR CALL

If you are ready for trial and you are willing to have your case heard by an Arbitrator....Answer: (Your Name), Ready

If you wish: to request a postponement of your case, to change the amount of the claim, or to add an additional party ......Answer: Your Name, Application

If you are ready for trial but you are not willing to have your case heard by an Arbitrator and you are requesting that the case be heard only by the Judge.....Answer: Your Name, Ready by the Court.

RESULT OF NON-APPEARANCE (DEFAULT)

If the Defendant (the person [being sued]) fails to answer or appear for trial an Inquest [hearing on damages] may be held. In an Inquest, the claimant must prove its case to the satisfaction of the

Arbitrator even though the Defendant is not present. In almost all instances the Inquest will result in a Judgment in favor of the Claimant.

If the [Claimant fails] to appear, the case will generally be dismissed.

Chapter 2
Some of the Other Small Claims Courts in the New York Metro area outside of New York City

Section 1 Nassau County

Nassau County publishes its own rules regarding commercial and non-commercial cases. See Appendix 2, <u>A Guide to Small Claims in District Court of Nassau County</u> (twenty-three pages). The relevant information from the Nassau County Rules is listed below:

Daytime Small Claims Parts (At: 9:30 A.M.)

Hempstead Part -- 2nd District - Civil Clerks Office, 99 Main Street, Hempstead, New York 11550 Telephone 516-572-2262

Great Neck Part - 3rd District 435 Middle Neck Road Great Neck, New York 11023 Telephone 516-571 -8400

Hicksville Past -4th District 87 Bethpage Road Hicksville, New York 11801 Telephone 516-571-7090

The Nassau Rules state, "If you wish to have your case heard in the daytime, you may file your claim in one of the three courts listed above. There is no limitation with respect to the selection of the court. Many plaintiffs choose to file in a court which is convenient to their home."

Night Small Claims:

Civil Part - 1st District
99 Main Street, Hempstead, New York 11550
Telephone 572-2262

The rules further state:

> You may initiate a night small claim at the Great Neck Part, Hicksville Part or the 1st District Part during normal business hours. The evening session is only conducted at 99 Main Street, Hempstead, New York, at: 6:00 p.m. on Tuesday, Wednesday and Thursday evenings. The judge calls the calendar at 6:00 P.M.

Other items to note in Nassau County as listed in the Nassau County Rules:

ARBITRATION

Arbitration of small claims cases is always available in the night small claims part and at times arbitrators are available to hear cases in the 3 daytime small claims parts.

If all of the participants to a small claims case consent they may have their case heard by an arbitrator rather than by a District Court Judge. The arbitrator is an experienced attorney who serves without pay and is appointed by the Supervising Judge of the District Court to act as an arbitrator. As with small claims trials held before a District Court Judge, a party may be represented by an attorney if his case is heard by an arbitrator.

If the parties agree to arbitration, each side will have the opportunity to give testimony, introduce evidence and have witnesses give testimony to prove their case or defense, as the parties and their witnesses will be under oath or affirmation, however, the arbitrator will not be bound by the rules regarding the admissibility of evidence. Under these circumstances, experience has shown that it is somewhat easier for a party to present their case or to defend themselves without being concerned about technical rules of evidence.

If the case is heard by an arbitrator, the parties will be bound by the decision and no appeal can be had from it. The arbitrator's decision, or award as it is known, is as binding upon all concerned as if it were a judgment of the court and as a matter of fact, when the arbitrator files the written decision with the court, it becomes a judgment of the District Court. It may then be enforced in the same manner as any judgment obtained after trial before a judge.

MEDIATION

At each small claims court location certified mediators are available to assist litigants in settling their case. The mediation sessions are non-judgmental and non-adversarial. Your appearance before a mediator is voluntary. If a settlement is agreed to, the mediator will prepare a written agreement detailing the terms and conditions of the settlement and will file it with the court. This agreement becomes a legally binding document. If after conferencing your case with a mediator, a settlement cannot be reached, you may return to the courtroom for trial.

Should you decide to go outside of the small claims system, the Nassau District Court hears cases seeking $15,000.00 or less.

Nassau County Sample Forms in this book:

Form 6 - Demand Letter

Form 11- Small Claims Complaint Form (non-commercial case)

Form 12- Commercial Claims Complaint Form

Chapter 2
Some of the Other Small Claims Courts in the New York Metro area outside of New York City

Section 2   Suffolk County

2nd District
375 Commack Road
Deer Park, New York 11729
631-854-1950
TOWN OF BABYLON
Wednesday Only; Day Court Only

3rd District
c/o 375 Commack Road
Deer Park, New York 11729
631-854-6726
TOWN OF HUNTINGTON
Friday Only; Day Court Only

4th District
North County Complex
Building C-158
Veteran's Memorial Highway
Hauppauge, New York 11788
631-853-5408
TOWN OF SMITHTOWN
Wednesday Only; Day Court Only

5th District
3105 Veteran's Memorial Highway
Ronkonkoma, New York 11779
631-854-9673
TOWN OF ISLIP
Tuesday and Thursday Day Court; Wednesday Night
Court

6th District
150 West Main Street
Patchogue, New York 11772
631-854-1440
TOWN OF BROOKHAVEN
Monday and Tuesday Day Court Only

The only evening court sessions take place in the Fifth
District Court in the Town of Islip

The Suffolk County District Court Complaint Form [FORM 13]

The top of the form contains spaces marked "for official
use only." These blanks include: Court, date, Index Number,
Time, Date Mailed. The rest of the form looks like this:

Check off one of the following:

Small Claims (Day)
Small Claims (Night)
Commercial Claim
Consumer Transaction

Plaintiff's Name Address and Zip Code. If plaintiff is a business you must use your true business name.

Defendant's Name Address and Zip Code. If defendant is a business you must use defendant's true business name.

Cause of Action (check one)

Personal Injuries
Property Damage
Loss of Personal Property
Goods Sold and Delivered
Breach of Contract or Warranty
Work, labor and Services
Monies Due
Payment of Loan
Refund on Defective merchandise
Refund on Defendant's Defective Work, Labor and/or Services
Action as Shown on Complaint Form

State Amount, Dates and Details:

The Undersigned acknowledges that he/she has been advised that supporting witnesses, account books, receipts and other documents required to establish the claim herein must be produced at the hearing. The undersigned further certified to the best of his/her knowledge, the defendant is not in the military service.

CERTIFICATION FOR COMMERCIAL CLAIMS ONLY (UDCA 1803-A)

The undersigned hereby certifies that no more than five (5) actions or proceedings (including the instant action) pursuant to the commercial claims procedure have been initiated in the courts of this state during the present calendar month.

Dated: (date to be filled in)

(Space for clerk or notary signature)
(Name of plaintiff)

What does the defendant receive? A Summons [FORM 14] that states the following:

Take notice that:
[Name of Plaintiff]

has asked judgment in this Court against you for $X.00 upon the following claim:

[MONIES DUE]

There will be a hearing before the court upon this claim on date and time at the _____ District Court, located at (address of Court).

You must appear and present your defense and any counterclaim you may desire to assert at the hearing at the time and place set forth above (a corporation must be represented by an attorney or any authorized officer, director or employee). IF YOU DO NOT APPEAR, JUDGMENT WILL BE ENTERED AGAINST YOU BY DEFAULT EVEN THOUGH YOU MAY HAVE A VALID DEFENSE. If your defense or counterclaim, if any, is supported by witnesses account books, receipts or other documents, you must produce them at the hearing. The Clerk, if requested, will issue subpoenas for witnesses, without fee thereof.

If you intend to file a COUNTERCLAIM against the plaintiff, you should file a statement containing the facts of the counterclaim with the Clerk of the Court along with the filing fee of $3.00 plus $.37 for each named plaintiff, within five (5) days of receiving this notice. NOTE: If you do not choose this method of filing a counterclaim, you may request permission from the judge at the hearing.

If you admit the claim but desire time to pay, you must appear personally on the day set forth for the hearing, and state to the Court your reasons for desiring time to pay.

DATE   Name of the Clerk
                        of the Court

NOTE: If you desire a jury trial, you must, before the day up on which you have been notified to appear, file with the Clerk of the Court a written demand for a trial by jury. You must also pay to the clerk a jury fee of $55.00 and file an undertaking in the sum of $50.00 or deposit such sum, in cash to secure the payment of any costs that may be awarded against you. You will also be required to make an affidavit specifying the issues of fact which you desire to have tried by a jury and stating that such trial is demanded in good faith.

Under the law, the court may award $25.00 additional costs to the plaintiff if a jury trial is demanded by you and a decision is rendered against you.

The Court also issues this information to the litigants as well:

ADJOURNMENTS
Requests for adjournments must be made in writing to the court with notice of the request given to all parties. Requests may also be made in person on the court date. No requests for adjournments will be accepted by phone. All requests for adjournments are submitted to the judge/arbitrator on the court date for approval. The court does not notify the parties of the new court date if the adjournment request is granted. You must contact the court to ascertain the new date.

PROOF OF CLAIM; DEFENSES TO CLAIM

On the court date you must submit all items necessary to prove the claim or to defend against the claim. Contracts, agreements, receipts, canceled checks, photographs and other documents should be produced at trial. Property damage may be proven by two itemized written estimates or by one itemized paid bill. Persons having actual knowledge of the facts and circumstances of the claim, or who are experts in a field may be present to testify. Expert witnesses cannot be subpoenaed to testify since most require compensation to appear in court.

DUTY TO PAY JUDGMENTS

(A) Any person, partnership, firm or corporation which is sued in a small/commercial claims court for any cause of action arising out of its business activities, shall pay any judgment rendered against it in its true name or in any name in which it conducts business. "True name" includes the legal name of a natural person and the name under which a partnership, firm or corporation is licensed, registered, incorporated or otherwise authorized to do business. "Conducting business" as used in this section shall include, but not limited to, maintaining signs at business premises or on business vehicles; advertising; entering into contracts; and printing or using sales slips, checks, invoices or receipts. Whenever a judgment has been rendered against a person, partnership, firm or corporation in other than its true name and the judgment has remained unpaid for thirty-five days after receipt by the judgment debtor of notice of its entry, the aggrieved judgment creditor shall be entitled to commence an action in small/commercial claims court against such judgment debtor, notwithstanding the jurisdictional limit of the court, for the sum of the original judgment, costs, reasonable attorney's fees, and one hundred dollars.

(B) Whenever a judgment which relates to activities for which a license is required has been rendered against a business which is licensed by a state or local licensing authority and which remains unpaid for thirty-five days after receipt by the judgment debtor of notice of its entry and the judgment has not been stayed or appealed, the state or local licensing authority shall consider such failure to pay, if deliberate or part of a pattern of similar conduct indicating recklessness, as a basis for the revocation, suspension, conditioning or refusal to grant or renew such license.

Nothing herein shall be construed to preempt an authority's existing policy if it is more restrictive.

Final note: Should you decide to go outside of the small claims system, the Suffolk District Court hears cases seeking $15,000.00 or less.

Suffolk County Sample Forms in this book:

Form 13 Suffolk County Complaint Form

Form 14 Commercial Claims Summons

Chapter 2
Some of the Other Small Claims Courts in the New York Metro area outside of New York City

Section 3 City Court of White Plains

City Court of White Plains
77 South Lexington Avenue
White Plains, New York 10601
914-422-6050

THE RULES APPEAR in Appendix 3, <u>A Guide Small Claims Court, New York State Unified Court System</u> (thirteen pages);

The Court uses a simple one page form: **[Form 15]**

Application Form

Check One   ___Small Claims
                ___Commercial Claim
                ___Consumer Transaction
                ___Counter Claim

Plaintiff Info:

Defendant Info:

Amt. Claim is for:

Briefly state reason for claim: (to be filled in.)

Signature of Claimant _____

If claim submitted via mail, Signature must be Notarized.

COMPLETE THIS SECTION FOR COMMERCIAL CLAIMS ONLY
I certify that no more than five (5) actions or proceedings (including the instant action or proceeding) pursuant to the commercial claims procedure have been initiated in the courts of this state during the present calendar month.

COMPLETE THIS SECTION FOR CONSUMER TRANSACTIONS ONLY
I hereby certify that I have sent a demand letter to _____defendant, at least 10 days, but no more than 180 days, before commencing this action.

What will the defendant receive? [FORM 16]

The City Court of White Plains summons states the following:

TAKE NOTICE the above plaintiff(s) seek judgment in this Court against you for $__ together with costs, upon the following claim:

[The court inserts a short statement based on the claimant's information]

THERE WILL BE A HEARING before this Court upon this claim on [date] at____ p.m. in the Small Claims Part [x], held at the above address.

YOU MUST APPEAR and present your defense and any Counterclaim you may desire to assert at the Hearing at the time and place set forth above (a corporation must be represented by an attorney or any authorized officer, director or employee). IF YOU DO NOT APPEAR, JUDGMENT WILL BE ENTERED AGAINST YOU BY DEFAULT, EVEN THOUGH YOU MAY HAVE A VALID DEFENSE. If your defense or Counterclaim, if any, is supported by witnesses, account books, receipts, or other documents, you must produce them at the Hearing. The Clerk, if requested, will issue subpoenas for witnesses, without fee. IF YOU ADMIT THE CLAIM, BUT DESIRE TIME TO PAY, YOU MUST APPEAR PERSONALLY ON THE DAY SET FOR THE HEARING.

IF YOU DESIRE A JURY TRIAL, you must before the day upon which you have been notified to appear, file with the Clerk of the Court a written demand for a trial by jury. You must also pay to the Clerk a jury fee of $____ and file an undertaking in the sum of $____ or deposit such sum in cash to secure the payment of any costs that may be awarded against you. You will also be stating that such trial is desired and demanded in good faith. Under the law, the Court may award $___ additional costs to the plaintiff(s) if a jury trial is demanded by you and a decision is rendered against you.

NOTE The Court does not encourage adjournments. Only the Judge may grant an adjournment request. All requests MUST be in writing with notice to the other party and for good cause. If you do not receive notice of a new date you or someone on your behalf MUST appear in Court to explain to the Judge why you cannot be ready for trial.

A defendant if he wishes to file a counterclaim shall do so by filing with the clerk a statement containing such counterclaim within 5 days of receiving the notice of claim. At the time of such filing the defendant shall pay to the clerk a filing fee of $___ which is required pursuant to this subdivision. The clerk shall forthwith send notice of the counterclaim by ordinary first class mail to the claimant. If the defendant fails to file the counterclaim in accordance with the provisions of this subdivision, the defendant retains the right to file the counterclaim, HOWEVER the counterclaim may, but shall not be required to, request and obtain an adjournment to a later date. The claimant may reply to the counterclaim, but shall not be required to do so.

BRING THIS NOTICE WITH YOU AT ALL TIMES!

A COPY OF THE BOOKLET, "A GUIDE TO SMALL CLAIMS PART" IS AVAILABLE AT ANY CITY COURT.

The plaintiff will receive a document [FORM 17] that states in part:

FAILURE TO APPEAR MAY RESULT IN THE DISMISSAL OF YOUR CLAIM(S)

INSTRUCTIONS TO PLAINTIFF - PROOF OF CLAIM

THERE IS A SPECIAL RULE OF LAW WHICH DISPENSES WITH THE NECESSITY OF HAVING AN EXPERT WITNESS (SEE ITEM D FOR EXCEPTIONS) TO TESTIFY IN CASES WHERE A PARTY IS SEEKING TO PROVE THE AMOUNT OF MONEY SPENT FOR REPAIRS AND/OR SERVICES OF ANY KIND WHEN THE REPAIRS AND/OR SERVICES HAVE BEEN COMPLETED AND THE BILLS ARE FULLY PAID. SEE ITEM A.

A. IF YOU HAVE A SIGNED ITEMIZED BILL

A signed itemized paid bill must be filed ten (10) days prior to the hearing with notice to the other side by certified mail.

B. IF YOU HAVE ESTIMATED BILLS

If you have only one (1) estimated bill, you must have your expert witness in Court to testify on your behalf, at the hearing.

C. IF YOU HAVE TWO (2) ESTIMATED BILLS

If you have not paid for the repairs or services pursuant to your claim, you must submit two (2) itemized estimates from two (2) different experts as to the reasonable value for those repairs and/or services. If this is the case, you will not need an expert witness in the court to testify on your behalf at the hearing.

D. IF YOU ARE CLAIMING
DEFECTIVE WORKMANSHIP
AND/OR MATERIALS, YOU MUST
HAVE YOUR EXPERT WITNESS IN
THE COURT ON THE HEARING
DATE TO TESTIFY ON YOUR
BEHALF

City of White Plains Sample Forms in this book:

Form 15 Complaint Application Form

Form 16 Commercial Claims Summons

Form 17 Notice to Plaintiff

Chapter 2
Some of the Other Small Claims Courts in the New York Metro Area Outside of New York City

Section 4 The General Rules of all the Small Claims Courts

If your case is outside the New York Metro area, the rules that apply to your case are the general rules for the Small Claims Courts. THE GENERAL RULES OF ALL THE SMALL CLAIMS COURTS APPEAR in Appendix 4, A Guide Small Claims Court, New York State Unified Court System (thirteen pages). However, you may want to look at the other Court Rules for additional ideas and to understand common themes that appear throughout the New York State Small Claims Court System.

Appendix 1, A Guide for the Use of the Commercial Claims Part, New York State Unified Court System (nine pages);

Appendix 2, A Guide to Small Claims in District Court of Nassau County (twenty-three pages).

Appendix 3, A Guide to Small Claims Court: New York City, Nassau County, Suffolk County 2001-2002 (thirty-three pages)

Chapter 3
Strategies for All Cases

Section 1 Counterclaims

What is a counterclaim? When the defendant or debtor countersues the person who has filed a claim, that action is called a counterclaim.

> Example: Let's say you are a self-employed car mechanic, and a customer comes in for an engine repair. You change the fuel injector, but the client refuses to pay you because the car's rear fender was damaged while the car was in your parking lot. You, the mechanic, will sue the car owner for the fuel injector and the car owner will file a counterclaim for vehicle body damage.

Sometimes defendants file worthless counterclaims thinking that they can somehow reduce the claim. This is misguided because a bogus counterclaim only infuriates the Court. It also proves that the debtor just does not want to live up to his or her obligations.

Just as the person who brings a claim has the burden (responsibility) for proving that claim, so does the person bringing the counterclaim.

Practice tip: A legitimate counterclaim is a sign that you should seek to settle your case.

ALWAYS CHECK TO SEE IF YOU NEED TO PAY A FEE TO
THE COURT IN ORDER TO FILE A COUNTERCLAIM OR
ASSERT A COUNTERCLAIM AS PART OF YOUR
DEFENSE.

Chapter 3
Strategies for All Cases

Section 2 Understanding Evasive Debtor Behavior

Make sure you have sued the properly named defendant. Why is this such a concern? Because in many instances, the claimants do not know the true legal name of the defendant in question. In some instances, debtors try to conceal their correct identity in order to dodge lawsuits and collection efforts.

How do Debtors Evade Creditors? By using a name in their invoices or letterhead that does not exactly match the name that appears on their certificate of incorporation (an example of such a certificate appears as FORM 4) or the title of their bank account.

If the debtor is not incorporated (a name that includes the words "Inc.", "Ltd.", or "Corp."), you may be able to sue the president individually but make sure that the company is not a Limited Liability Corporation (known as L.L.C.'s) or a Limited Partnership (L.P.). When in doubt, seek legal advice from an attorney.

Chapter 3
Strategies for All Cases

Section 3 Documenting Your Claim

The best way to document your claim is to send a "final" demand letter to convey your intentions and to establish a clear written record. Many clients send these letters by certified mail, return receipt requested, in order to have absolute proof of delivery.

The Nassau County District Court provides a blank demand letter which appears in this book as FORM 6 and it could be used as a model of a demand letter for your Small Claims Cases filed in other Counties.

Chapter 3
Strategies for All Cases

Section 4 Should I contact the defendant in the interim?

There can be a significant time delay between the date you file your claim, and the assigned trial date. Many claimants ask whether they should write or call the defendant to see if the case can be settled during this interim period. The claimant should not initiate any communications with the defendant prior to the trial.

If you have sent a number of invoices or written demands for payment without an adequate response (i.e., partial payment, credit, or adjustment), then the initiation of a lawsuit will probably not motivate your debtor to pay prior to trial.

In some instances, the debtor will contact you to work things out or to complain that you are not owed the money. If you receive a communication from the defendant that payment will not be made, listen carefully. You will be learning the debtor's potential trial defenses. In order to successfully litigate your claim, you should be prepared to respond to the numerous defenses the debtor may offer as a defense of the debt. These defenses often include the following types of excuses:

- Someone else is responsible for payment (the classic "**not me**").

    If there is even a hint of truth to this defense, you may need to think about adding additional defendants into your case to make sure you have all the potential debtors gathered together in one lawsuit. It is better to find this defense out BEFORE you file the small claims case since there is tremendous difficulty in adding a defendant into an already existing lawsuit. Since there is no procedure for consolidating cases or amending a complaint in the small claims court rules, it may be simpler to withdraw the initial action and bring a new suit with all the correct parties. The best advice is to make sure you sue everyone before you bring the action.

- The debt was not incurred by someone authorized by the business to act on its behalf.

    This is a variation of the preceding excuse. You may need to sue an additional party.

- There is no "budget item" for the alleged debt.

    This is basically a non-answer and has no meaning in a Court of Law.

- The debtor has run out of cash/has a cash flow problem/is going out of business.

    A common problem. This is why so many creditors demand personal guarantees.

- The creditor waited too long to file the claim.

    The statute of limitations on a debt in New York State is six years from when the debt was due (CPLR 213). However you need to be aware that there are ways to reduce this six-year time period. For example, a contract may state that there is a shorter period of time to bring a lawsuit than the one made by the New York State legislature. This is known as a <u>contractual limitation</u> and may be a valid defense. Insurance companies often take advantage of this contract technique. Make sure to read all of the contractual terms if there is a written contract. When in doubt, contact an attorney to determine your rights.

- The creditor's price was too expensive.

  Translation: the debtor is looking for a bargain.

- The amount sought by the creditor is not the amount that the parties agreed to.

  Another common issue. Check your facts and records. The lesson to be learned is to confirm everything in writing for the next time. A hard lesson taught repeatedly in the business world.

- The creditor did not fill out the right form or application.

  Translation: the debtor does not want to pay.

- We required a competitive bid and this Project was not put out for bid.

  Translation: the debtor does not want to pay.

- The amounts the creditor seeks are part of the base contract and are not "extras."

  One of the most common issues in the construction industry especially in cases involving home improvement.

- The creditors thought you volunteered to undertake the task at no charge since we did not ask for it.

  Yes - this is argued in Court on occasion.

- There is nothing in writing so we will not be paying you.

  A nonsense defense. A contract can exist through a course of conduct over time, or a writing can be constructed from various documents. Most important, a payment by a debtor will "ratify" (confirm) a contract. If you are given this defense, just bring the best evidence you have to trial and argue your case.

Sometimes the reality is that the debtor simply does not want to pay you. Other times, the debtor will not pay you because the debtor is waiting for funds from someone else and is stalling. Either way, you want to be paid and to some extent, the excuse is meaningless to you. However, there is a real psychology to debt. Many times debtors get into jams because they are not precise in their records or their business activities. You need to understand the psychology of the debtor you are dealing with in order to determine your course of action. If the debtor is so aggressive in defending the suit or becomes "super-technical," it may prompt you to hire an attorney if the amount sought is significant.

Chapter 3
Strategies for All Cases

Section 5   Powerful Evidence and Detailed Backup
Documentation

In terms of business, New York is a demanding town. I
never really appreciated how tough New York is until I started to
represent out-of-town clients in New York actions. I remember
what the President of a construction equipment leasing firm said
in a Court proceeding, "My business operates in sixteen states,
and the only problems we have with collection occur in New
York."

In the past, my law firm served as the New York Counsel
for a nationwide medical concern. The representation at times
was contentious because of real business cultural differences. In
New York, all the defendants fought every case vigorously. The
reason why there was so much opposition to these particular
lawsuits was because none of the contracts at issue were in written
form. (In other jurisdictions a simple handshake is considered
binding on the parties.) When I told the client that the Courts
always want to know what the contract stated, the national
counsel said, "we don't have that problem in other states." The
bottom line: No one has ever suffered because there was too much
proof or too much backup documentation in their favor.

What we must learn from experiences like these is that you
must have as much proof and detailed backup documentation as
possible. The lack of reliable evidence will only serve to diminish
your case. The best tactic in litigation is to be in a position of
strength. Documents that are signed by the debtor give you the
strength you need in Court.

Great Evidence Paves Your Way to Success

Sometimes, before the Court hears a case, the parties are asked "What is this case about?" This is your opportunity to give an informal opening statement. Imagine when you confidently give the following summary to the Court: " Your honor, I had a signed, written contract with the defendant to provide equipment at the rate of $2,000 per month. The debtor had the equipment for 3 months, evidenced by copies of their checks written to my firm, but failed to pay the last rental. I have my dispatcher here to testify and I brought all the delivery and pickup tickets from my office to prove my claim. I am ready to proceed."

An opening statement must be concise, comprehensive, and bottom line. It also must project strength, organization, and attention to detail.

After summary statements, the Court may ask one of two important questions:

(1) "Have the parties discussed settlement?" or

(2) "Does the defendant need a payout plan?"

These words are exactly the kinds of statements you want to hear because this shows that the Court realizes that you should win and that the problem is not liability but the defendant's ability to pay.

Evidence Acquired From Your Opponent through the Service of a Subpoena

In most cases, the best evidence comes from your own files and from your business records kept in the ordinary course of your business. However, there are times when your adversary or a third-party is in the "exclusion possession" (sole control) of documents and/or testimony. To obtain this information, you need to serve a subpoena. Since the rules for the gathering of this type of evidence can be complex, I have included in this section the rules regarding subpoenas taken directly from the Court rules. The procedures for the service of a post-judgment information subpoena upon a bank (or any other entity that owes money to the debtor) are different and are separately discussed in the section dedicated to collecting money after you are awarded a judgment.

SUBPOENA RULES AS PUBLISHED BY THE COURT- New York City cases only

The following rules were published by the Civil Court of the City of New York.

This information is available for <u>free</u> from the New York City Civil Court Clerk's Office. Check with your local Court to make sure you have a copy of the latest rules, and to make sure that these rules apply to you or your case.

If you have any questions, please consult an attorney.

INSTRUCTIONS FOR SERVICE OF SUBPOENA

There are three kinds of Subpoena,

I. Subpoena To Testify. (Ad Testificandum) Requires a person to come to the Court to testify as a witness.

II. Subpoena For Records. (Duces Tecum) Requires documents, papers, writing, etc. to be brought to the Court.

III. Information Subpoena.
Requires that information be provided to the person requesting it.

Methods of Service

A Subpoena to Testify or a Subpoena for Records is generally served on an individual* by personal (in hand) delivery. [For service on a partnership or on a corporation, see instructions below.] If the individual is not available, under certain circumstances it may be appropriate to use an alternate method of service such as "Substituted Service" or "Conspicuous Service."

"Substituted Service" is the personal service of the Subpoena on someone other than the person who is being subpoenaed (the witness) at the actual place of business or place of residence of the witness.

The server must then mail a copy of the Subpoena to the witness by first class mail to the actual place of business or place of residence of the witness. Mark the envelope "Personal and Confidential"

"Conspicuous Service" is the service of the Subpoena by leaving it at the residence or place of business of the witness. Prior to leaving the Subpoena, the server must make at least two attempts. If no one is found on either attempt, on the third try the Subpoena may be affixed to the door with adhesive tape, and a copy must be mailed
to the residence of the witness by first class mail. Mark the envelope "Personal and Confidential."

An Information Subpoena is generally served by Certified or Registered Mail, Return Receipt Requested, or it may alternatively be served by personal delivery or by using the

"Substituted Service" or "Conspicuous Service" method.

Who May Serve a Subpoena

Anyone NOT A PARTY to the action, who is over the age of 18 and not a Police Officer, may serve the Subpoena.

Proof of Service

The person who serves the Subpoena to Testify or the Subpoena for Records must fill out an Affidavit of Service and have it notarized.

Procedure

The person who is going to serve the Subpoena must:

1) Find the person to be served.
2) Show that person the original Subpoena.
3) Give that person a copy of the Subpoena.
4) Fill out the Affidavit of Service on back of the original.
5) Retain the Affidavit of Service for further procedures if the person fails to comply with the Subpoena.

For an Information Subpoena, follow the above procedure, or

I) Place a copy of the Subpoena, together with an original and copy of the questions to be answered and fifty cents ($0.50)*[A person served with an Information Subpoena must be paid a fee of fifty cents ($0.50). However, no fee need be paid to a Judgment Debtor for responding to an Information Subpoena in an envelope addressed to the witness.] [Author's note: no fee is needed if the subpoena is sent to a bank.]

2) Include a self-addressed, stamped envelope for use by the witness returning the answered questions to you.

3) Mail the envelope to the witness by Certified or Registered Mail, Return Receipt Requested.

Fees for Service

When served with a Subpoena to Testify or a Subpoena for Records, the witness must be paid a witness fee of $15.00 per day. If the witness is served outside the City of New York s/he shall also be paid 23 cents per mile to the place of attendance, from the place where s/he was served, and return. The fee must be paid a reasonable amount of time before the scheduled date. Nonpayment of the witness fee voids the duty to appear.

Location

A Subpoena from the Civil Court of the City of New York may be served only within the City of New York or in Nassau County or Westchester County. Service anywhere else in New York State may only be done if permitted by a Judge.

Restrictions

General

A Subpoena may not be served on a Sunday.

A City or State agency or a public library may be subpoenaed only by order of the court.

Time

Any witness must be served a "reasonable" amount of time prior to the date of appearance. It is suggested that service be at least 5 days before the date of the hearing.

A City or State agency or a public library must be served at least 24 hours prior to the time of appearance.

* Service on a Partnership or Corporation

A Partnership may be served by delivering the Subpoena to any of the partners.

A Corporation may be served by delivering the Subpoena to an officer, director, managing or general agent, or cashier or assistant cashier or to any other agent authorized by appointment or by law to receive service. In this context "cashier" normally means "treasurer" of the corporation, not one who operates a cash register.

Citation: CIV-GP-63 (Revised 6/92)–designation given by the Civil Court of the City of New York. Please check as these rules may have been revised especially with respect to fees.

SUBPOENA RULES AS PUBLISHED BY THE NASSAU COUNTY COURT

Source: Appendix 2 pages 11-12

If your prospective witness will not or cannot appear voluntarily, you should visit the court where the trial as scheduled and request the form entitled "Application for Subpoena." Please note that a subpoena cannot be issued until the defendant has been served the summons. This may be determined by calling the clerk's office. You should file the "Application for Subpoena" form at least ten (10) days before your trial date, as it takes several days for the clerk's office to process your application and prepare the subpoena. There is no charge for this service. The subpoena with instructions for its service will be mailed to you. The court does not serve subpoenas. Please be advised that the person who serves the subpoena will have to pay the witness a $15 fee plus round-trip mileage of 23 cents per mile.

Our final word regarding subpoenas. The court cannot subpoena your own "expert' (i.e. mechanic or medical provider). You may very well have to pay your "expert" whatever he requests for his time to appear and testify in your behalf.

Chapter 3
Strategies for All Cases

Section 6   What to Expect at Trial

The best way to settle a case is to be ready for trial.

Settlement

It is always better to settle than to litigate. Even when you have overwhelming evidence, the Court may issue a ruling that you find unfair. Sometimes the defendant makes 100 excuses why you or your firm should not be paid. The list is endless, but the popular ones are "I did not order the equipment/product/service," I asked for X and got Y, the service/equipment was substandard, I was overcharged, the item was broken, the plaintiff misrepresented X, Y and/or Z, and/or delivery was late.

Settlement should be interpreted as a victory for the claimant because the claimant will be receiving some money without further controversy. Settlement agreements are generally in writing, and should contain a provision that if the defendant fails to make a payment, then a judgment shall be entered in favor of the plaintiff for the full amount of the claim less any payments made to the creditor/claimant.

Every Court treats settlements differently so check your local rules. The New York City and Nassau County rules regarding settlement are listed below:

> The New York City Rules Regarding Settlement
> Specifically State:
>
> > If you and the Defendant are able to work
> > out a settlement, the written agreement

(Stipulation of Settlement) should be filed with the Court. This should be done on or before the date set for the Hearing. The document provided to the Court must include the Small Claim Number of your case and the year. (Note: this is known as the "index number.")

If the Defendant admits the claim but desires more time to pay, and you are not willing to accept the plan for payment, you must appear personally on the date set for the Hearing. At that time, with the aid of the Court, you may be able to reach agreement on the terms of payment.

The Nassau County Rules Regarding Settlement Specifically State:

If you have settled your case before the day of trial and received your money, you should promptly notify the court by mail of that fact. If you have not received the money by the day of trial you should appear as if no offer of settlement has been made at all, otherwise your case might be dismissed.

If you receive an offer of settlement on the day of trial which you decided to accept but the defendant does not have the money with them to pay you or you would like additional time to consider the offer, you should inform the judge of the pending settlement and he will adjourn the case to a future day "subject to settlement." If the defendant does not pay you, or you decide not to accept the offer, then come to court on the adjourned date and be prepared to proceed to trial. If payment is made, both parties should notify the court by mail so the case can be recorded "settled' on the adjourned date. (Nassau County Rules p. 15.)

Practice Tip: If you are the party paying the debt, make sure to write something to the effect that you are making payment in full and that no other monies will be due to the creditor. You should make this statement on both the front and back of the check you are issuing to the claimant. A suggested phrase that you could use:

This check constitutes full payment for any and all debts from A to B. Deposit of this check constitutes a full release from B to A. This payment also completely resolves the lawsuit between A and B filed in ____ County under index number _____.

What does a settlement agreement look like?

A sample settlement agreement from an actual case (with the names changed) appears below:

<u>Sample Settlement Agreement</u>

Civil Court of the City of New York
County of New York: Small Claims Part

John Smith

                    Claimant

                                              Index 7654321/2001

                  -against-

                                              STIPULATION OF
                                              SETTLEMENT

John Jones

                    Defendant

This action is settled as follows:

1.   This action is settled for a total of $2,000.00 (two thousand dollars and no cents).

2.   Plaintiff acknowledges partial payment in the amount of one thousand dollars and no cents paid on or about June 15, 2001 (reference: certified check 0505 paid by Jones to Smith).

3.   The remaining one thousand dollars shall be paid as follows: ten payments of one hundred dollars due the 1st of each month commencing July 2001.

Thus payments are due for the following months:

> July 2001
> August 2001
> September 2001
> October 2001

November 2001
December 2001
January 2002
February 2002
March 2002
April 2002

4. All payments (by good check, certified check, money order or bank check) shall be made payable to "John Smith" and sent to John Smith at 1313 Mockingbird Lane, Apt 607, New York, New York 10023.

5. Default: should defendant deliver a bad check or any check that is dishonored by a bank, or fail to make a timely payment, a default shall be declared by claimant. Such default will be noticed by Plaintiff who will send a certified letter to defendant declaring the default. Defendant shall have 10 days from the date of the certified mailing to cure the default by paying the amount past due (plus an additional $30.00 to cover the bank fees if any.) If the default is not cured within these 10 days, plaintiff shall have the right to enter a judgment WITHOUT FURTHER NOTICE for $1,000.00 (one thousand dollars and no cents) LESS any payments made after June 25, 2001 plus costs of $100.00. Interest shall accrue from June 25, 2001.

6. For the purposes of having a clear record, the defendant's address is 1 Gillligan's Island Plaza, # 4G, NY, NY 10128.

7. The Judgment Clerk is directed to enter judgment in accordance with this stipulation IF there is a default which shall be evidenced by a copy of the certified mailing. Plaintiff shall not need any additional proof as a prerequisite for entering a default judgment.

Agreed to:

_____   _____
John Smith plaintiff   John Jones, defendant

SO ORDERED:

_____
Date: June 25, 2001

See also FORM 5 for a blank NYC stipulation of settlement form.

Chapter 3
Strategies for All Cases

Section 7 The Basics Rules for all Trials

1. Do not appear late.

This may sound obvious, but appearing late could mean that your case has been marked off the calendar if you are the plaintiff, and even worse, if you are the defendant, you may have automatically lost (in which a default judgment will probably be entered against you.) In either event, restoring the case to "active" status is a major pain.

2. Know the rules.

If you are unsure about the Court's procedural rules, read the rules very carefully. The Court and its operations are all governed by specific procedural rules. You must follow these rules even if they seem a bit at odds with common sense. For example, the Court generally requires affidavits (sworn statements) of service (i.e., delivery upon a party) attached to certain types of documents such as subpoenas commanding the production of witnesses and/or documents to the trial.

3. Bring original documents to Court.

The Court wants to see the original copies of invoices and contracts. Maintain your originals in a safe place and bring them to Court. It is a good idea to give the Court copies of documents while explaining that you have the originals with you and are prepared to produce them for inspection.

> Practice Tip: Never permanently surrender your original documents which are unique and irreplaceable.

4. Be organized.

Bring your documents in an organized file and be ready to present your case in a logical sequence. Use chronological order if possible in order to establish a time line. Bring a large file folder with clearly marked subfolders containing four copies of each document. (One for you, one for the Court, one for the adversary, and one extra for perhaps a Court reporter.)

Appear professional. Have legible copies and whenever possible typed documents. Speak clearly and loudly--generally the acoustics are quite poor. You are in Court to be heard, do not miss this vital opportunity.

5. The Calendar Call-New York City Cases. Prior book reference: chapter 1 section 6

The Calendar Call can be confusing. As a result, the process will be explained in full detail including your options and the phrases the Court employs in its cases. Knowledge gives confidence which in turn makes you more effective.

When you arrive at the Court, see if your case is posted on a bulletin board or on some master list. In some Courts, such as the White Plains Small Claims Court (Westchester County), you check in before the official Calendar Call, and inform the Clerk that you are present and ready to proceed or that you require an adjournment. The Clerk will then mark the list accordingly. In some counties, cases are called on the basis of those who checked in first.

If the cases are on a master list posted outside the Courtroom first check the date of the list. Sometimes the list is for a prior night. Look to see if your case is listed. Write down the number of the case and the name of the calendar. (For example your case may be number 19 on the commercial calendar, or number 43 on the adjourned calendar if this is a second appearance.)

If your case is not on the Calendar, double check your receipt to make sure you went on the correct evening. In the New York City Small Claims Courts, you cannot ask any questions about your case until the entire calendar has been called. If there is a Clerk's office that is open, try that first, but it is unlikely that there will be any office open to help you. In that event, see if your adversary is present (that is a good sign) but in any event wait for the Calendar Call to conclude. At this point in time the Clerk will say "if you did not hear your case called or if you have any questions please form a single line."

If your case is on the Calendar you must answer in one of the following ways in the New York City Commercial Courts:

Plaintiff Ready
Plaintiff by the Court
Plaintiff Application

Defendant Ready
Defendant by the Court
Defendant Application

When you say "Ready" you are informing the Court that you are willing to have a volunteer attorney act as an impartial arbitrator and decide your case. The benefit of this situation is that your case will be heard that evening. There is no appeal from the decision which is good because your case will be finished one way or another.

When you say "by the Court," you are insisting that only the Judge will hear your case.

Chapter 3
Strategies for All Cases

Section 8 "Lack of Service" also Known as Failure to Serve a Defendant with the Complaint

There will be times when the Clerk will call the name of your case: Spacely Sprockets v. Cogswell Cogs, and you will stand up and say PLAINTIFF READY. The Clerk then may say to you that the "service of process" was defective. (Translation: the certified mail sent by the Court to the defendant was not claimed or was sent back to the Court as "undeliverable" by the Post Office.) You now bear the burden of having to hire a process server to serve the complaint personally upon the defendant. Ask the Clerk for instructions on how to proceed. You will not be granted a default because you must serve the defendant before you can qualify for a default judgment.

The lack of service upon the debtor (the failure to get the complaint into the hands of the debtor through the Clerk's certified mailing) will force you to decide whether it makes sense to go forward. Double check your facts.

> Did you use the correct name of the defendant?
> Is the address current and correct?
> Does the defendant reside at more than one location?

A process server can cost sixty dollars or more. If your information is incorrect and you now know the correct information, it may be cheaper to file a new small claims law suit. On the other hand, if the address is correct, and the defendant is merely "ducking" service, you will have to hire a professional company to serve the complaint and fill out an affidavit declaring that the process server actually served the complaint. An example of this type of affidavit appears as FORM 18.

The law does not permit you to serve the complaint yourself because you are a party to the action. In fact, affidavits of service filed in the Courts in New York State begin with the phrase, "I am over the age of 18 and I am not a party to this action." If you are ambitious or intellectually curious, the Service of Process Rules can be found in the New York Civil Practice Law and Rules (CPLR) sections 306 and 308.

If you need assistance locating a process server, try the Internet or the Yellow Pages. You can also find out who the Process Servers are by visiting the Civil Court's main Clerk's Office. I found the Process Servers my law firm uses by meeting a Process Server waiting on a long line in Queens Civil Court. I asked the gentleman for his card and kept it on file. If you know an attorney, ask for a recommendation.

Note: Never interrupt the calendar call. This is when the Clerk reads out loud the names of the cases while at the same time determines whether the parties are present and ready for trial. Every once in a while, during the Calendar Call, a litigant has a question. (They did not hear their name, a name was mispronounced etc.) and the litigant moves closer to the clerk to ask a clarifying question. Upon their approach to the Clerk at the Bench, the individual is always admonished. Bottom line: Wait until the call is over before you approach the Clerk.

Chapter 3
Strategies for All Cases

Section 9   Trial Before an "Arbitrator" (a volunteer attorney)

Trial before a Volunteer Attorney

The New York City Small Claims Court system is able to process cases because of the volunteer efforts of experienced attorneys. They are called arbitrators, but they really make decisions as if they were a judge. They will issue a decision on the outcome of your case in the form of a judgment. See FORM 9. The only difference between a trial before a judge and a trial before this type of volunteer attorney is the right to appeal the decision. Once you agree with your opponent that an arbitrator will preside over your case, you also agree not to appeal the decision. However, appeals are only recommended in very rare circumstances so this is a good avenue to take to resolve your case whether you win or lose.

Every arbitrator has a different style of presiding over the case. Some are very formal, others cut into the discussion and try to get the essential information immediately. This is no different from the way various judges conduct their trials.

Trial before a Judge

In the New York City Small Claims Court system you can insist on having your case heard before a judge. However, because the number of judges available per session is quite small and the case load vast, your case will be delayed when demanding a trial before a judge. Defendants use this tactic to drag out a case and make it unpleasant for the plaintiff. But in the end this behavior is never rewarded by the Court. The Court wants settlement, not delay.

So the question is, when is it appropriate to insist on having your case tried before a judge as opposed to a volunteer experienced attorney? <u>The major reason is to preserve your rights to appeal if you lose</u>. However, the appellate process in all cases, including small claims court, is complex. In the small claims context, an appeal is almost never really worth the effort and only should be done with the assistance of an attorney.

When else is it appropriate to have a trial before a judge? In the limited situations when the enforcement of technical procedural and evidentiary rules is important. This will be rare. If your case requires such attention to minute details, then you really should think about hiring an attorney.

The only other set of cases that require a judge are those cases that have consequences in other Court cases. For example, if you win in small claims court, you can then later on in a subsequent case sue someone personally on a guarantee. Again, if the stakes are that high, obtain guidance from an attorney.

Chapter 4   How to Conduct a Trial

It is important to explain the facts in a concise manner and in chronological order using documents to support your case. If possible, ask for a one minute opening statement to provide an overview of your case and the amount due.

Your opening statement should be restricted to raw provable facts. For example: Good evening, I am Bob Smith, President of the Acme Company. The defendant, Greedy Miser, Inc., hired my company, an equipment rental company, based on a written contract to provide certain tools rented monthly. The defendant paid all of our invoices except the last two which amount to $2,200.00. This amount has been past due for over 15 months.

If you have a lot of documents, more than fifteen, purchase a loose-leaf binder and number each separate document as an individual exhibit. You will need three copies of each set of exhibits: one for you, one for the Court, and one for the adversary.

Common misperception: many claimants believe that the defendants should not be given any copies of documents at trial because they "should already have them." This is not how the evidence system works. Bring copies for the defendant and the Court to read at the same time. It will show that you are thorough and organized.

Make sure to bring the original copies of all documents since the Court or your adversary may want to inspect these items.

> Practice tip: Store your originals in your briefcase and only pass out copies unless directed to do so. Once the adversary has finished reviewing the original document, demand the return of your original document. The Court is treated differently. The Judge or arbitrator generally holds all original documents throughout the proceeding.

At the end of the trial make sure to take all of your papers with you.

Most commonly asked question: I do not have any original documents since I gave them to the debtor at the time of the transaction.

Answer: your original documents are any copies containing an original signature (known by attorneys as documents containing "blue ink" signatures regardless of the color of ink used) or the best copies contained in your business files or personal possession. Thus, in an invoice system where two copies are created, and one copy is mailed and the other copy is retained by the front office, the office file copy is considered an "original."

Another commonly asked question: My office does not keep any written invoices on file since everything is on the computer. What do I do to satisfy the Court's request that I bring original documents?

Answer: Explain that your records are all computerized and bring a complete printout of the computer document to the Court. You must provide testimony to accompany the document so that someone can state that the copy " IS A TRUE AND CORRECT COPY " of what is contained in the computer and what was transmitted to the debtor. If you cannot make this statement under oath, bring the person to Court who can make this statement. By the way, the words "true and correct copy" are the specific words the Court looks for so make sure to use this phrase.

The Outcome or Trial Decision: The Court almost never issues its decision while the parties are present. One reason is to keep order in the Court because at least one party will "lose" and not be happy about it. Sometimes, both sides are disappointed in the result.

Before your trial or inquest, the Court officers will ask you to fill out your address (and the address of your non-appearing adversary in a default) on official pre-printed addressed business size envelopes. The decision will be mailed to you.

If you do not receive a decision in the mail after three weeks, I suggest that you contact the Clerk's office to find out the status of your case. In general, the Clerk maintains copies of all written decisions.

Court Records

Given space limitations, the Court will archive older case files. Check to see if your files are in the active files or archived records room. Archived records may have to be requested in advance of the time you need them since it may take several days for the Court system to retrieve them.

Chapter 5   How Not to Conduct a Trial

Do not to make any of these common trial mistakes:

1. Arguing with the Court or interrupting the Court while the Judge or Arbitrator is speaking.

2. Shouting

3. Cursing

4. Making accusations that do not seem to be realistic. Example, you agreed to purchase a brand-new luxury car for only $2,500.00.

5. Not providing documents that should be considered as a business record. Example: not providing an original or copy of your real estate broker license when you are claiming to be an active, licensed broker.

6. Presenting disorganized or conflicting evidence that contradicts your case or aspects of the case. For example, you assert in one document (such as an invoice) that the defendant owes one amount, but your contract with the debtor is for a different amount. Make sure you have an explanation for this difference. For example your plumbing contract with a debtor home owner is for $1,800.00 but your final invoice is for $2,200.00. If the reason for the difference is additional work generated after the contract was signed, make that clear. The Court is always concerned that damage claims are inflated by the claimants for wrongful purposes. (Wrongful purposes include many categories but people seem to add extra amounts to "compensate the claimant for time in Court" which is never recoverable.)

7. Giving really long explanations when a concise statement would have been sufficient.

8. Inflating charges hoping that the Court will find a compromise number close to the actual amount due.

9. Outright lying.

10. Disregarding Court rules.

11. Suing the wrong defendant or the correct people under the wrong name.

In order to illustrate how the Court views the litigation process, I have interviewed an experienced, Small Claims Court volunteer attorney, and asked the following questions:

Interview with a Small Claims Court Volunteer Attorney Who Decides Cases (name withheld to preserve confidentiality and identity)

Question 1: What was the most common mistake made by small claims litigants in commercial cases?

> Answer: "Failure to bring proof of the amount of damages they had. Even when I believe they are telling me the truth, I cannot award damages unless they show me the value of the item that was damaged, lost etc. You will be surprised at the amount of people who come in without any proof."

Question 2: What could plaintiffs do before going to Court to improve their chances of winning?

> Answer: "Document their loss. It would definitely help if they at least sent the defendant a letter prior to commencing an action."

Question 3: What upsets you the most as a finder of fact?

> Answer: "That some people have no problem lying straight to you. I am not talking about stretching the truth or puffing a bit. I am talking straight out lying."

Chapter 6   Advanced Trial Tactics

This section goes beyond the basics and offers a few practice tips in advanced strategy.

Advanced Tactic Number 1: Using partial payments by the debtor to prove your claim

If you have a case in which the debtor has made a partial payment, you can use the payment as evidence of the debtor's agreement that you are owed money. In legal terms this is called "ratification of a contract" since the act of payment ratifies (confirms) the debt. This is why you should always make copies of checks you are given as payment.

Advanced tactic Number 2: Using partial payment to prove a settlement which is a new contract

You can also seek to enforce a settlement agreement by using this strategy because a settlement is a new contract by definition (as long as a partial payment was made). Thus, whenever a debtor agrees to settle a case and makes at least one payment, you can use the settlement agreement as a new contract and sue for the non-payment of that contract.

Example:

Creditor lent some money to a roommate in Manhattan. The debtor used the money to retrieve her automobile from the New York City Sheriff's Department. At the time, she was extremely grateful and wrote out in her own handwriting a promise to repay the debt. She made partial payment then disappeared. After a number of years, the creditor decided to sue before the statute of limitations expired. The defendant debtor defaulted and a judgment was issued after the small claims court conducted a hearing on the damages known as an inquest.

The creditor kept the judgment for a number of years and then called an attorney friend to see what could be done about collecting the judgment. The attorney served a subpoena on her employer and gave this information to the City Marshal with instructions to garnish her wages. The debtor decided to fight the debt (even though the evidence was to the contrary) hoping to vacate the default judgment.

After two Small Claims Court appearances, the debtor realized that it would be best if she settled. The offer was for a settlement of $2,000.00 payable as follows: $1,000.00 immediately and ten payments of one hundred dollars. In support of this agreement, the debtor sent this letter:

> I am enclosing the $1,000.00 certified check as we agreed to as partial payment toward the overdue loan.
> /signed the debtor

The significance of the settlement agreement is that it created a new contract that was ratified and made it unnecessary for the creditor to justify the original default judgment.

When it came time to inform the Court of the settlement, the debtor once again changed her mind about paying this new debt and decided to see if either the new debt (the settlement) or the old debt (evidenced by the default judgment) could be avoided trying a new theory of why the money was not really owed at all. (Maybe someone encouraged her to fight the case which in hindsight was bad advice from a legal and factual standpoint).

The Court (during a third conference) realized that the debtor was trying to back out of a ratified contract casting doubt as to the debtor's credibility. The Court showed its displeasure by reprimanding the debtor and the set the case for immediate trial. This move by the Court convinced the debtor to accept the terms of the settlement or face a loss on the original debt which was a larger amount and carried with it years of interest.

Advanced Tactic Number 3: Motivating the Court to initiate settlement

The Court encourages settlement in order to dispose cases. If you are before the Judge (and not the volunteer arbitrators) and the trial is about to begin, the best time to initiate the concept of settling is after a Court official has asked what the case is about. Before you go to the waiting area to be called for trial, ask if the Court can talk privately to the parties to see whether a settlement can be achieved before trial.

Most times, the Court will see this as an opportunity and will work hard on reaching a settlement between the parties. If the other side appears unreasonable, the Court will see that you made a good faith effort to resolve the dispute and the other side did not. In a close case, this may mean the difference between winning and losing.

Advanced Tactic Number 4: <u>Wording the Settlement Agreement in Your Favor</u>

What should a settlement agreement contain?

Settlement agreements are critical documents. Draft your agreements carefully. List everything you have agreed upon including dates when payments must be made to someone. Always add terms to enforce the debt if the creditor does not get paid by the date payment is due. If you are the debtor, make sure to obtain a release of liability or some other acknowledgment that the debt is no longer due once final payment is made.

Form 5 is the form generally used in Manhattan Small Claims Court for settlements approved by the Court.

The key term to include if you are the claimant is a paragraph that explains what will happen if the debtor does not make a settlement payment or issues a bad check. For example:

(Use language similar to what appears below.)

<u>Default</u>: should defendant deliver a bad check or any check that is dishonored by a bank or fail to make a timely payment, a default shall be declared by claimant.

Such default will be noticed by plaintiff who will send a certified letter to defendant declaring the default. Defendant shall have 10 days from the date of the certified mailing to cure the default by paying the amount past due (plus an additional $30.00 to cover the bank fees if any.)

If the default is not cured within these 10 days, plaintiff shall have the right to enter a judgment WITHOUT FURTHER NOTICE for $1,000.00 (one thousand dollars and no cents) <u>LESS</u> any payments made after (insert date) plus costs of $100.00. Interest shall accrue from (insert date).

The Judgment Clerk is directed to enter judgment in accordance with this stipulation **if** there is a default which shall be evidenced by a copy of the certified mailing. Plaintiff shall not need any additional proof as a prerequisite for entering a default judgment.

This format provides clear guidelines as to what will happen should the debtor fail to make the promised payments to the claimant. Mark this page for easy reference in Court, and should you settle your case, adapt the model language into your settlement agreement. The Court will not provide any guidance to you on how to draft a settlement document.

Chapter 7   Inquest – the Hearing to Determine Damages

Many claimants ask, "How do I present evidence at a hearing to prove my damages when the defendant fails to appear? The best way to illustrate the techniques in presenting evidence in a hearing to prove damages is to provide a claimant with a transcript of an "Inquest on Damages." The following transcript is taken from a Supreme Court case in Queens. Although this is not from a Small Claims Court case, it illustrates the dynamics of live testimony.

The names of the parties have been changed to "creditor" and "debtor" and non-relevant material has been deleted to conserve space. If you are alone, you will testify in a monologue format stating the same content but without the questions and answers. If you have brought a witness such as a bookkeeper, you will ask the questions and your witness will respond.

Court transcription taken from an Inquest: (Q=Question, A=Answer)

Q.   Please tell us your employment and title.

A.   I am vice president of credit and risk analysis for the creditor.

Q.   Are you familiar with the account of the debtor?

A.   Yes.

Q.   What is your understanding?

A.   From the period December 1998 through about March 1, 1999, they purchased fuel from us and have not paid the invoices we sent to them.

Q.   Did you bring the invoices with you today?

A.   Yes.

Q.   Did debtor ever make payments to your company?

A.   Yes.

Q.   What were the forms of their payments?

A.   Either check or wire transfer.

Questioner: If I may your Honor, I would like to introduce into evidence as Exhibit 1, copies of the checks paid by debtor if the witness will be kind enough to hand the copy to the Court.

The Court: Deem it marked.

Q: Very briefly, what are we looking at?

A: Example of a check we received from the debtor on December 4, 1998.

Q: Now you brought some invoices with you?

A: Yes.

Questioner: We marked the original invoices as Exhibit 2.

The Court (to the witness): Is it your testimony that all the books of this account, that everything that was billed was for fuel that was actually delivered?

A: Yes.

The Court: And the sum of $X.00 represents all amounts billed for all fuel delivered to the defendant less credited for the amounts paid by the defendant?

A: Yes, your Honor.

The Hearing ended and an award was issued. Please note that the Court will ask questions during the exam to expedite matters. If you are prepared and brought all your evidence, the Inquest should go smoothly.

Chapter 8 Judgment

Section 1 The Basics

A Judgment is a Court generated document specifying the monetary winner(s) and loser(s) of a litigation. A copy of a small claims judgment appears as FORM 9. (Note that it is generally one sheet, double sided.)

Listed below are two important laws concerning judgments. This list is not comprehensive; rather, it highlights some important issues to take into consideration.

Civil Practice Law and Rules (CPLR)
Section 5011: Definition and Content of Judgment

A judgment is the determination of the rights of the parties in an action or special proceeding. . . . A judgment shall refer to, and state the result of, the verdict or decision, or recite the default upon which it is based. * * *

Section 5016: Entry of judgment
(a) What constitutes entry. A judgment is entered when, after it has been signed by the clerk, it is filed by him.

A judgment grants the winner the right to enforce the judgment. However, you cannot simply "grab" the money or property. There are specific procedures you must adhere to. Before you can enforce your judgment, you must survive any challenge to your judgment if it was taken by default (the failure of the defendant to appear). The most common challenge is when you obtain a default judgment, and the defendant informs the

Court that the summons and complaint were never received. The process is called vacating a default judgment, and is discussed in the next chapter of this book.

Chapter 8 Judgment

Section 2 Vacating Default Judgments-an overview

More often than you think, defendants fail to appear in Court to defend the action. When that occurs, the Court will conduct an inquest (a determination) of damages. The claimant will present the case without any opposition. If the Court agrees, and they usually do, the claimant will be awarded a default judgment.

This judgment can be taken to a Sheriff or Marshal to execute against the assets of the non-appearing defendant. When the defendant learns that the Marshal is on the job, the defendant will run to the Clerk's office seeking to vacate (remove) the judgment. Since this is such a common occurrence, the Clerk has a preprinted form for this type of procedure. To the dismay and shock of most claimants, this motion is almost always granted by the Court. Should the judgment be vacated, you will have to go back to Court and this time have both parties argue their case.

The step-by-step procedure: The defendant fills out two forms: an affidavit in support of an Order to Show Cause (FORM 19) and an Order to Show Cause (FORM 20). The Clerk will instruct the defendant on how the document should be transmitted to the claimant. The Order will have a Court appearance date on it in which both sides are to appear.

The parties will appear in Court where the Court will almost always vacate the judgment. The Court policy is to decide the cases on the merits which is why they will order a new trial even though the defendant did not appear in the first instance. This does not really appear to be fair, but it is the reality of the Court system. What a claimant should do in this instance is try to obtain as many concessions against the defendant as possible such as (1) have the trial date marked as "final" against the defendant, (2) demand compliance with the production of documents or evidence in the exclusive possession of the defendant, (3) have the Marshal keep any money that may have been obtained as part of the default judgment enforcement process until the case is resolved. (This can be used as leverage to promote settlement.)

What Defendants Need to Say to Successfully Vacate (Remove) Default Judgments and What Should Claimants Expect.

If a judgment has been obtained by default, the defendant usually has the opportunity to make a motion to the Court to "vacate" the default judgment. This was explained in the preceding section of this book. The two basic elements the defendant must successfully assert in order to convince the Small Claims Court that the motion should prevail are:

> (1) service of process was either not made in accordance with the law, or that service was not made at all;
> -and-
> (2) the defendant has a defense that is "meritorious" meaning that it has merit.

CPLR section 5015 is the law governing this type of motion. This law states:

> **5015. Relief from judgment or order.**
>
> **(a)   On motion.** The court which rendered a judgment or order may relieve a party from it upon such terms as may be just, on motion of any

interested person with such notice as the court may direct, upon the ground of:

1.   excusable default, if such motion is made within one year after service a copy of the judgment or order with written notice of its entry upon the moving party, or, if the moving party has entered the judgment or order, within one year after such entry; or

2.   newly-discovered evidence (this does not relate to defaults so the remainder has been omitted from this guide.)

3.   fraud, misrepresentation, or other misconduct of an adverse party; or

4.   lack of jurisdiction to render the judgment or order; or

5.   reversal, modification or vacatur of a prior judgment or order upon which it is based.

(b)   On stipulation. The clerk of the court may vacate a default judgment entered pursuant to section 3215 upon the filing with him of a stipulation of consent to such vacatur by the parties personally or by their attorneys.

(c)   On application of an administrative

judge. (The remainder of this subsection omitted since this material does not apply in general to small claims court actions.)

(d)   Restitution. Where a judgment or order is set aside or vacated, the court may direct and enforce restitution in like manner and subject to the same conditions as where a judgment is reversed or modified on appeal.

I included the applicable law regarding this topic for two reasons. The first is that the law is not clear to non-lawyers so it will be explained below. The second reason is to have this law readily available in Court so that you can bring this section into the Courtroom with you to support or defend against a motion to vacate a default judgment.

What does this law, CPLR section 5015, really mean?

In section a, the law directs that there are five grounds to remove a judgment by motion. Only four of the five sections apply to default judgments. Essentially only one is relevant to every day small claims court cases. The other sections are included in order to fully understand how the Courts remove judgments.

The first ground to remove a default judgment is called "excusable default" but there are certain conditions. The motion must be made within **one year** of the service of the default. In general, an excusable default means you did not receive notice of the lawsuit or some other reason why you failed to appear such as you were in the emergency room when the Court appearance occurred and you were legitimately ill. Simply refusing to appear after having been properly served with process is never considered to be an excusable default.

The next ground, section 5015 (a) 3, concerns the fraud or other misconduct of the adverse party. This will depend on the facts, but this has to do with the fraud of the other party in obtaining the judgment. This has nothing to do with anyone's failure to pay or their bad faith in business activities. An example of this would be when an affidavit of service was forged or faked by the other side in order to obtain the default judgment.

The third ground, section 5015(a) 4 relates to the capacity of the court to issue a judgment in the first place. For example, you are a defendant and your office is officially registered in Delaware County, but your company was sued in Queens County. The default can be removed under this section because the Court did not have proper jurisdiction over the defendant because the defendant must reside within the 5 boroughs of New York City if the case was brought in Queens.

The final ground, section 5015 (a) 5 relates to some other proceeding upon which the current judgment is based. For example, in a landlord tenant action, a judgment is issued against the tenant for damages to a building. In the small claims action against the same tenant or someone who guaranteed the tenant's payment, a default judgment can be removed if the judgment in the original landlord tenant action was vacated.

In order to bring a motion to vacate a default judgment, the moving party must do so by "Order to Show Cause." Basically, this unusual phrase comes from the procedure that an order has been issued by the Court to the winner that the claimant must show cause (prove) why the judgment should not be vacated. (This is not a grammatical error, the motion is phrased in the negative.)

In almost every case, the Court will vacate a default

judgment. This seems unfair but the Court's rationale for vacating default judgments is that they strive to have all cases decided "upon the merits."

Some attorneys believe that devious defendants default on purpose only to make a motion brought on by order to show cause to frustrate the claimant. This aspect of the small claims litigation system needs to be reformed, but until that day arrives, be prepared to try your case immediately once the Court removes the default judgment.

Practice tip: The Order to Show Cause Hearing may be your best opportunity to settle the case. Ask the Court to promote settlement discussions between the parties. If all else fails, ask for a trial date as soon as possible, even if that means, trying the case right then and there. If the Court cannot conduct a trial at that moment, ask that the date selected be marked "final" as against the defendant.

Chapter 8 Judgment

Section 3 Enforcement of a Judgment

The hardest part of the small claims court process takes place when you are seeking to collect your money by "enforcing" your judgment. This is not hard to do from a procedural level. The obstacles you face come from the lack of information. To collect your money, you and the Sheriff or N.Y.C. Marshall must **locate assets** that can be seized by the Sheriff or Marshal in order to satisfy (pay) your judgment. This means that your focus now changes from litigation to investigation.

Accurate information will mean the difference between a successful collection and getting nothing.

Since it is up to you to supply as much information to the Sheriff or N.Y.C. Marshal as possible to make their job easier, it is time to put on your detective hat. The best asset to locate is a bank account. This is because an account can be seized without great difficulty by the enforcement authorities. Other assets such as motor vehicles need to be sold by the Sheriff or N.Y.C. Marshal before you can receive the money. (The authorities will not give you the debtor's vehicle or property. Generally those items are sold at a public auction.)

When a vehicle is sold, the cost of advertising is born by the person forcing the sale. In addition, auctioneers receive a sales commission for the sale. Now you can see why bank accounts are best. When the enforcement officials seize an account on your behalf, they will deduct a fee against the money they have obtained. If the debtor has sufficient assets, this will not be a problem since this fee is taken from the debtor. If the amount seized is less than the amount hoped for, the creditor's "take" is reduced by the fee.

Example 1. You have obtained a $2,000 judgment against the debtor. Debtor's bank account has $3,000. The Marshal's fee is 5% (or $100). Thus, the Marshal will collect $2,100 from the debtor, keep $100 as "poundage" (the fee) and mail a check to you for $2,000. This example was simplified by neglecting to discuss interest which keeps increasing against the debtor as time goes on. Also, to commence the enforcement process, you will need to give the Sheriff or N.Y.C. Marshal a fee up front.

Example 2. You have obtained a $2,000 judgment against the debtor. Debtor's bank account has $900. The Marshal's fee is 5% (but here it is only $45). Thus, the Marshal will collect $900 from the debtor, keep $45 as "poundage" (the fee) and mail a check to you for $855. This situation is called a "partial satisfaction of judgment" which means that you are still owed money. If you can find other assets, you are entitled to go after those assets until your judgment is fully satisfied as long as it is within the time period allowed by law to collect on the judgment. For our purposes here, it is ten years. There are technical rules to extend this time period, but if you cannot collect your money in ten years you will probably never collect at all.

Locating the Debtor's Bank Account

There are several methods that you can try in order to determine the identity of the debtor's bank account. First, try to find any copies of checks recently issued by debtor. This will tell you the name of the Bank and the debtor's account number. If those materials are not available, see if anyone you know sent a check to the debtor for payment. Look at the back of the canceled check to see where it was cashed.

Second, the law allows you to serve an information subpoena and restraining notice on banks. See FORM 21 (**this form is for N.Y.C. cases only**). The form for cases outside N.Y.C. must be purchased from a legal supply store but check first with the local Clerk's office. To narrow the list of all banks down to the ones where the defendant most likely has an account, try to figure out which banks are located near the debtor's residence. Most people bank for convenience. Use this knowledge to make a list of potential banks to serve with an information subpoena.

Locating Other Assets

Most assets are subject to seizure. Examples include motor vehicles and boats registered in the name of the debtor. Accounts receivable for businesses and wages for individuals are other assets that can be attacked.

Once the assets are "located," you will then need to go through the steps necessary to seize these assets. The Nassau County Rules offer information that details the enforcement process that I find quite helpful:

Enforcement of a Judgment–the Specific Nassau County Rules

THE JUDGMENT HOW TO COLLECT IT–page 17 of the rules (Appendix 2)

After the trial or inquest, the court will notify the parties of the Judge's decision. This is known as the judgment. It will inform the parties either:

1.   That the plaintiff is awarded judgment against one or more defendants in a specific amount of money, or,

2.   that the defendant is awarded judgment dismissing the plaintiff's claim, and/or

3.   that the defendant is awarded judgment against the plaintiff on defendant's counterclaim in a specific sum of money.

If, after obtaining a judgment you do not receive your money, within a reasonable amount of time (2 - 3 weeks) from the judgment debtor, it is advisable to contact the debtor. If the debtor informs you that he or she does not intend to pay, or you receive the impression that the debtor is avoiding the obligation to pay, or you are unable to reach the debtor after several attempts to do so, you should take steps to obtain an execution. An Execution is a legal document which authorizes the sheriff to collect the judgment amount for you.

You can assist the Sheriff in collecting your judgment by providing information identifying property of the judgment debtor. The identity of the defendant's bank account is a most valuable bit of information to furnish the Sheriff.   Is the defendant employed? Does he or she own a car? Source of income-what are they? Answers to these questions are important if the Sheriff is to succeed in the pursuit of the judgment debtor's assets. If you obtain information of this nature, put it in writing and furnish it to the Sheriff at the time the execution is requested.

There is a law that will give you further assistance in identifying the debtor's assets. The law provides that if after you are awarded a judgment, it remains unsatisfied, the court clerk will assist you in the preparation of an information subpoena. An information subpoena is a legal document commanding the judgment debtor or some other person to answer questions about the debtor's assets and income.

The person served with the information subpoena is required to answer these questions in writing. (Author's note: the equivalent N.Y.C. court form appears as FORM 21.)

The court clerk has information subpoena forms and instructions for this purpose and will assist you in the preparation of these forms and furnish you with written instructions concerning their service and what to do with the information once it is obtained. There is a $2.00 fee for an information subpoena.

Examples of questions commonly asked in an information subpoena to be served upon a judgment debtor are

What is the name and address of your employer?

What are your weekly earnings?

What is the name and address of your bank?

What is your savings account number and the balance of that account?

Examples of questions commonly asked in an information subpoena to a bank are:

Does the judgment debtor maintain an account in your bank?

What is the account number and balance of that account?

To obtain an execution you should first request the court to issue a transcript of judgment. A $5.00 fee is charged for issuing a transcript. After obtaining the transcript you should file it with the Nassau County Clerk and request that an execution be issued to the Sheriff of Nassau County. Both the Nassau County Clerk's and the Sheriffs office are located in the corner building at 240 Old Country Road, Mineola, New York 11501.

You have the right to notify the appropriate state or local licensing or certifying authority of an unsatisfied judgment if it arises out of the carrying on, conducting or transaction of a licensed or certified business or if such business appears to be engaged in fraudulent or illegal acts or otherwise demonstrates fraud or illegality in carrying on, conducting or transaction of its business.

In addition, if the judgment debtor has two (2) prior unpaid judgments of a small claim court, which arose from the judgment debtor's trade, business, or from a repeated course of dealing or conducting business, you (judgment creditor) may have the basis for an action for treble the amount of your judgment. (Author's note" treble" means triple.)

Additional reference: Appendix 4, A Guide to Small Claims Court, pages 9 through 15.

The Step-by-Step Process of Asset Seizure

To start the process of collection, you will need to provide the Sheriff or N.Y.C. Marshal with certain forms that can be **purchased** at a legal supply store. **A list of the Sheriff's offices in New York State sorted by County appears as part of Chapter 9 of this book.** These forms are **not** free and are **not** provided by the Court. A company known as Blumberg Excelsior ® sells these pre-printed forms and the Sheriffs' and N.Y.C. Marshals' offices will tell you which form (by its numbered designation) they require.

There is a difference between the different the types of assets that can be seized. When a physical (tangible) asset is attacked, the process is called a "property execution."

When going after a bank account (an intangible asset) you or the enforcement authorities must first restrain the account (which is sometimes called freezing the account). The next step is when the authorities execute upon the account also known as a levy. The levy is where the money is extracted from the account.

Of all the assets that exist either tangible or intangible, the best asset to go after is a bank account, so that topic will be discussed first.

Bank Account Seizure-the step-by-step process

The ideal way to collect your judgment is to freeze a bank account that has the same exact name (the technical term is "title") as the party you have the judgment against. This is accomplished by serving a "Restraining Notice" on the bank.

Your first question: what do I serve? Due to copyright restrictions, I cannot insert a copy of the Blumberg Excelsior ® form in this book because this is not a form created or supplied by the Court, but a privately published form used quite frequently in the litigation system.

> In New York City, request Small Claims Court form number 60 from the Clerk [see Form 21 in this book] and follow those instructions if you wish to do the initial work without the assistance of the Marshal or Sheriff. However, the execution against the account (the taking of the money) is only done by the enforcement authorities and never by the creditor. So in essence, it is probably best to have the Sheriff or Marshal help you at every step of the process. They are expert at what they do and can be very helpful.

The company that sells this privately published Restraining Notice form is called Blumberg Excelsior ®. There is no alternative vendor for this form, and the Court system will not aid you in creating this form for you. Please take notice that the author and publisher do not recommend or endorse this company or their products. This information is provided because this is the way the system works at present. If you call them on their 800 number, they will tell you the store closest to your home or office to purchase their forms. Their contact information is 800-529-6278 [1-800-law-mart] and www.blumberg.com on the internet.

The Restraining Notice is a one sheet document directed to someone holding the assets of another (such as a bank) with the directive that they are to freeze the amount of the judgment. The notice describes the name of your case, the date of the judgment, the amount awarded and still owed (usually this is the same amount) and some description of the debtor' s assets.

How to fill out the Pre-Printed Restraining Notice Form

Most frequently asked question: Do I need to type onto the form? No, but it is preferred. If you fill out the form using your best handwriting, be as neat as possible. If the bank cannot read your handwriting, they will reject your form or misinterpret the information and may give you an incorrect result.

In the top of the document you must fill in the caption: the name of the plaintiff and defendant(s), the index number.

Where the form says "To" on the top, **insert** the name of the bank.

Where the form states:

"Whereas, in the action in the _____ court of _____ county of _____ between _____ as plaintiff(s) and _____ as defendant(s) who are all parties named in said action, a judgment was entered on _____in favor of _____ in the amount of _____ of which _____together with interest theron from _____ Whereas, it appears that you owe a debt to the judgment debtor or are in possession or in custody of property in which the judgment debtor has an interest:

you should fill in the blanks as follows:

"Whereas, in the action in the <u>Small Claims</u> court of <u>the</u> county of <u>New York (Manhattan)</u> between <u>Joe's Plumbing, Inc.</u> as plaintiff(s) and <u>Mike's Tiles Corporation</u> as defendant(s) who are all parties named in said action, a judgment was entered on <u>(insert the date of the judgment which should be the trial date)</u> in favor of <u>Joe's Plumbing</u> in the amount of (the exact amount listed in your judgment, for example $3,000.00) of which $3,000.00

together with interest theron from (insert the date of the judgment)

Whereas, it appears that you owe a debt to the judgment debtor or are in possession or in custody of property in which the judgment debtor has an interest:

Any and all bank accounts under the name Mike's Tiles Corporation.

If you know the bank account number or the tax identification number insert that information on the form as well.

Place your name and address on the bottom and date the document. Now, before you sign the bottom, make spare copies for your file (at least two). Now take one copy and sign it.

How to Serve the restraint on the Bank

Most frequently asked questions:
How do I know which bank to pick?
Do I need a process server?

Selecting the Bank

How do I find out the debtor's bank account information? You may actually have this information in your files. Check to see whether a check was issued by you or your company to the debtor. If the check was cashed, the account information is on the reverse side. Similarly, if the debtor has ever issued a check and you kept a copy, you will know the bank name, branch, title of the account, and account number.

Practice tip : Keep photocopies of all incoming checks as a matter of information gathering.

If you do not have this information, try to find out if you know anyone who has done business with the debtor. Maybe they have the information on a credit application or in their files. One other possibility is to find out the banks located within a few blocks of the debtor's offices. Most people bank close to their homes or offices so that should narrow down the list of potential banks.

Your final option is to hire an asset location company. Please research these companies thoroughly before hiring them. What do they promise, what will they give you, how long will it take, and how much should it cost are your first questions.

Assuming you know the identity of the bank, the easiest way to serve the bank is to hand deliver a copy of the pre-printed Restraining Notice along with a copy of the judgment to the bank. Bring an extra copy with you and have the bank stamp somewhere on the extra copy that they received a copy of the Restraining Notice. Please request a business card of the bank official you met. **Do not deliver the notice to the tellers**. When you serve the restraining notice, ask for the telephone number of the bank office that will process your documents.

The bank officer will then forward the notice to their legal department or some central office where restraints are processed. One bank calls this department "legal holds and levies."

In the past, I recommended to my clients that they include a copy of another pre-printed form called an Information Subpoena, but now most banks generate their own form and mail that material to you. Ask the bank what forms or documents they require to process your request.

The bank will not provide any information over the telephone regarding your success or failure in locating an account. Assuming you are successful, you will receive a written response from the bank. Generally, the bank freezes twice the amount of the judgment.

If you were awarded a judgment against "Road Rage International, Inc." You can only restrain accounts under that name. You certainly cannot restrain the account of the owner UNLESS you have a personal judgment against the owner as well.

Secret weapon!

Under section 332 of the New York State Vehicle and Traffic law, the Commissioner of Motor Vehicles is authorized to suspend the driver's license or registration of any person or company who fails to pay a judgment of more than $1,000.00 that results from the use or operation of any motor vehicle. Thus, if you have sustained property damage from a car accident, go to small claims court and obtain a judgment for greater than one thousand dollars and it remains unpaid, seek to have the debtor's license suspended. For more information contact the New York State Department of Motor Vehicles, Insurance Services Bureau, 6 Empire State Plaza, Albany, New York 12228-0330. (website: www.nysdmv.com)

If all else fails, try an "income execution." This is when the Sheriff or Marshall deducts a percentage of a person's income only when the judgment is against an individual. Because the rules are complex, please discuss this option with the officials who will be assisting you in this effort known as an "income execution" or a "garnishment of wages." There are other methods of trying to pressure debtors such as notifying a license issuing authority, but use this tactic as a last resort. Just so you know, page 11 of Appendix 3, A Guide Small Claims Court, New York State Unified Court System (thirteen pages) states:

If the judgment debtor is engaged in a business that is licensed or certified, you may notify the appropriate state or local authority if the judgment remains unpaid 35 days after the judgment debtor receives notice of entry of the judgment. The failure to pay a judgment may be considered by the licensing authority as a business for the revoking, suspending, or refusing to grant or renew a license to operate a business.

Chapter 8   Judgment

Section 4 Paying a Judgment (known as a "satisfaction of judgment")

If you are on the paying end of the transaction, you will want to prove that you have paid the judgment in full. This is known as a "satisfaction of judgment." If you are paying a judgment, you should ask for some documentation to prove your payment for several reasons. The first is to completely close the matter with the Court system. The second is to show the satisfaction of judgment on any credit report. This will be your best and perhaps only opportunity to obtain this documentation. You should also save your canceled check as further proof of your payment.

In addition, make sure to send a cover letter to your adversary that states essentially the following:

Dear Mr. Laurel:

Enclosed please find the following 4 items:

(1) a check in the amount of $400.00;

(2) a satisfaction of judgment which needs to be signed before a notary;

(3) a general release which also needs to be signed before a notary; and

(4) a self-addressed stamped envelope.

Please return items 2 and 3 in the return envelope. Thank you. If you have any questions, please call me.

Please further note that I wrote on the check: This check constitutes full payment for any and all debts from [name of debtor] to [name of creditor]. Deposit of this check constitutes a full release and satisfaction of any judgments.

Very truly yours,

Mr. Hardy

Practice Tips: The Satisfaction of Judgment and General Release are preprinted, fill in the blank forms available from a private company sold in stores that carry these forms. The Court will not supply these forms and neither will your adversary. The cost is relatively small.

If you pay the creditor less than the full amount and the creditor accepts this amount as payment in full, you will be entitled to a full satisfaction of judgment. However, sometimes the creditor wants the entire amount of the judgment and will not accept any less. Remember no one is obligated to settle.

If you pay in part because of a sheriff's execution, you are entitled to have the Court records reflect that the judgment is **partially** satisfied. The problem with a partial satisfaction is that interest keeps running on the balance and the creditor will use whatever means is necessary to collect the full amount.

Thus, it is always better to settle in Court and pay that amount if you believe you will not prevail at trial.

Chapter 9   You Win Some, You Lose Some

We are now at the nitty gritty of debt collection, the potential seizure of a bank account. After you serve the restraining notice, you may learn the following:

> "Information Supplied is not sufficient to process this document. [meaning your restraint]. If you have additional information, please resubmit for further processing."

Generally this response is issued when you do not have a social security number or tax payer identification number for the bank to conduct its search. Sometimes, the name you have is slightly different from the one listed for the account. Sometimes the address you supply is different from the one on file. Other times, sophisticated debtors use an invalid tax identification number. Several years ago, my office noticed that in one of our cases, the debtor company used the social security number of its president instead of its federal tax identification number.

Never underestimate the cunning of a debtor corporation to hide its assets. I have seen instances where debtors kept their business in New York but had their bank accounts in Connecticut. This is done to defeat collection efforts because a New York judgment can only be enforced within New York State. To seize money in a Connecticut bank that has no branches in New York State, you will have to start a suit in Connecticut to enforce the New York judgment. Since this book is about small claims, it will almost never be worth hiring an out-of-state attorney to collect your New York judgment in another state. In fact, some States do not honor default judgments.

Another classic debtor trick is to have two different corporations with similar names located at the same address. My office once discovered that a certain company used the names

ABC MOVING for its business, but maintained its assets under the name ABC CONTAINERS.

Practice Tip: Always double check the debtor's information before you sue. If its too late in your current situation, look at checks the debtor may have issued or deposited. Locate other businesses that have worked with or for the debtor. Use your networking skills and develop a sense of sleuthing.

Another statement that may accompany the return of your documents:

> "A search of our records indicates that there are no assets in the name of the Judgment debtor. These responses are based upon a search of data contained in the (name of bank) central computer system that may not necessarily capture all relevant information concerning the judgment debtor(s). . . ."

If the debtor had an account, even one that was overdrawn, you would not receive this statement. Double check your information on the debtor. You may have the wrong bank. For example, there are two different banking institutions in New York that contain the word "Dime."

The statement you want to see may look like this:

> In order to expedite a response to your Information Subpoena/Restraining Notice, we are using this method of reply.

Pursuant to the restraining notice served upon the Bank, a hold has been placed on the judgment debtor(s) account(s).

Account Title: ABC Enterprises general account
Account type: checking
Account number: 1234567
Balance status: $2,500.00
TIN [tax payer identification number] - 12-3456789

This is exactly what you want to see. It has been my experience that immediately after monies are restrained, the debtor will call you. Sometimes they are angry and say things like "we could have worked this out," but you know that it is not genuine.

This is the only opportunity where you will have power over the debtor. Generally, the bank freezes twice the amount of the judgment. This is done to cover Marshal/Sheriff fees (five percent) and possibly interest that has accumulated.

If the debtor wishes to settle, this is the opportunity. **Do not let them trick you into releasing the money so they can write a check to you**. Instead, work out a deal with the debtor and have the debtor instruct the bank to issue a check directly to you from the frozen bank account. You will need to confirm this with the bank since the bank has no interest in becoming an intermediary in your dispute with their customer.

If the Marshal or Sheriff is not involved at this point, you do not have to pay their fees. Instead, you will need to send a letter to the bank that states the following:

ABC Creditor Corporation v DEF Debtor Inc.
Kings County Small Claims Court Index No. 89101112/2002

Dear [name of bank official]:

In accordance with my agreement with Mr. Joe Jones, president of DEF Debtor Inc., account number jzx-8978893b, please issue a check for twenty-five hundred dollars and no cents ($2,500.00) payable to "ABC Creditor Corporation" out of the restrained funds and mail it to me at my office address listed above. (Please also refer to Mr. Jones' letter which will be sent under separate cover authorizing this release of funds.)

Based on the foregoing, please **release** to DEF Debtor Inc., any other funds that you may have under the restraint issued by my company.

If you have any questions or need further documentation, please call me immediately. Thank you.

Very truly yours,

Joe Jones, President

Marshals and Sheriffs

In New York City, both Marshals and Sheriffs are available to assist you in the collection of your judgment. Since the Sheriff's department generally is extremely busy, I often choose a City Marshal who is a private sector employee authorized by the City to execute against bank accounts, personal property, and income.

The Marshals and Sheriffs earn their fees in one of two ways. First, you provide an initial fee to commence an activity in their office. The second way comes from "poundage." The Marshal or Sheriff will take five percent of the amount seized from the debtor to satisfy the poundage. When the debtor has more than enough assets to satisfy the debt, the poundage is an extra surcharge against the seized assets. However, if there are insufficient assets to pay the judgment, the five percent is deducted from that amount.

Practice Tip for Outside New York City:

In general, the Sheriff's department is the office you must contact once you have obtained a judgment and need to collect upon it. The Sheriffs departments are located in the government blue pages of the telephone directory. In addition, your local Court may be able to provide this information to you.

Some downstate Sheriff offices and their telephone numbers:

Manhattan
Surrogate's Court Building
Room 608
31 Chambers St.
New York, New York 10007
212-788-8730, 212-788-8731

Queens
144-06 94th Avenue
Jamaica, New York 11435
718-298-7500

42-71 65th Place
Woodside, New York 11377
718-803-3091

Bronx
332 E. 149th Street
Bronx, New York 10451
718-585-3164

Staten Island
350 St. Mark's Place
Room 202
Staten Island, New York 10301
718-815-8407 or 718-876-5308

Brooklyn
210 Joralemon St.
Brooklyn, New York 11201
718-802-3545 and 718-802-3543

Nassau
> 240 Old Country Road
> Mineola, New York 11501
> 516-571-2113

Suffolk
> Civil Bureau
> 112 Old Country Road
> West Hampton, New York 11977
> 631-852-8000

Westchester
> 1 Saw Mill River Parkway
> Hawthorne, New York 10532
> 914-741-4440

When transacting with the Sheriff's or Marshal's offices, I suggest that you telephone their office first, find out if they can assist you, the amount of the initial fee, and the forms and quantity of original documents and copies they require. Each office has its own procedures, so its best to find out from the office that will be enforcing your judgment.

Directory of local Sheriffs outside the New York City Metro region

Due to budget issues, security concerns, and changes in area codes, please make sure that these addresses and phone numbers have not changed since the publication of this guide. Internet addresses, if available, are listed as well.

Albany County
16 Eagle Street
Albany, New York 12207
518-487-5400

Allegany County
7 Court Street
Belmont, New York 14813
585-268-9200

Broome County
Justice Building
Binghamton, New York 13902
607-778-2492 or 1911

Cattaraugus County www.sheriff.cattco.org
County Center
301 Court Street
Little Valley, New York 14755
716-938-9111

Cayuga County
Public Safety Building
County House Road
P.O. Box 518
Auburn, New York 13021
315-253-1222

Chautauqua County
15 E. Chautauqua Street
P.O. Box 128
Mayville, New York 14757
716-753-2131

Chemung County
Justice Building
203 William Street
P.O. Box 588
Elmira, New York 14902-0588
607-737-2987

Chenango County
14 West Park Place
Norwich, New York 13815
607-334-2000

Clinton County
25 McCarthy Drive
Plattsburgh, New York 12901
518-561-1810

Columbia County
85 Industrial Tract
Hudson, New York 12534
518-828-3344 or 0601

Cortland County
Public Safety Building
54 Greenbush Street
Cortland, New York 13045-5590
607-753-3311

Delaware County
Courthouse Square
P.O. Box 326
Delhi, New York 13753
607-746-2336

Dutchess County
150 North Hamilton Street
Poughkeepsie, New York 12602
845-486-3800

Erie County www.erie.gov/sheriff
10 Delaware Avenue
Buffalo, New York 14202
716-858-7618

Essex County
100 Court Street
P.O. Box 278
Elizabethtown, New York 12932
518-873-3346

Franklin County
Courthouse
45 Bare Hill Road
Malone, New York 12953-1893
518-483-3349

Fulton County
2712 State Highway 29
P.O. Box 20
Johnston, New York 12095
518-736-2100

Genesee County
14 West Main Street
P.O. Box 151
Batavia, New York 14020-0151
585-343-3000

Greene County
80 Bridge Street
P.O. Box 231
Catskill, New York 12414
518-943-3300

Hamilton County
P.O. Box 210
South Shore Road
Lake Pleasant, New York 12108
518-548-3113

Herkimer County
County Office Building
320 North Main Street
P.O. Box 550
Herkimer, New York 13350-0749
315-867-1167

Jefferson County
753 Waterman Drive
Watertown, New York 13601
315-786-2600

Lewis County
Public Safety Building
Outer Stowe Street P.O. Box 233
Lowville, New York 13367
315-376-3511

Livingston County
4 Court Street
Geneseo, New York 14454
585-243-7120

Madison County
County Correctional Facility
Court Street
Wampsville, New York 13163
315-366-2289

Monroe County www.monroesheriffny.org
130 South Plymouth Avenue
Rochester, New York 14614
585-428-5780

Montgomery County
200 Clark Drive, P.O. Box 432
Fultonville, New York 12072
518-853-5515

Niagara County
P.O. Box 496
5526 Niagara Street
Lockport, New York 14095-0496
716-438-3370

Oneida County
Law Enforcement Building
6065 Judd Road
Oriskany, New York 13424
315-765-2222

Onondaga County
407 South State Street
Syracuse, New York 13202
315-435-3044

Ontario County
74 Ontario Street
Canandaigua, New York 14424
585-394-4560

Orange County
110 Wells Farm Road
Goshen, New York 10924
845-291-4033

Orleans County
13925 State Route 31
Albion, New York 14411
585-590-4137

Oswego County
39 Churchill Road
Oswego, New York 13126
315-349-3302

Otsego County
172 County Highway 33 West
Cooperstown, New York 13326
607-547-4271

Putnam County www.putnamcountyny.com
3 County Center
Carmel, New York 10512
845-225-4300 general number; 845-225-5550 civil process

Rensselaer County
4000 Main Street
Troy, New York 12180
518-270-5448

Rockland County
55 New Hempstead Road
New City, New York 10956
845-638-5400

St. Lawrence County
48 Court Street
Canton, New York 13617
315-379-2222

Saratoga County
6010 County Farm Road
Ballston Spa, New York 12020-0600
518-885-6761 general and 518-885-2269 civil process

Schenectady County
Schenectady County Jail
320 Veeder Avenue
Schenectady, New York 12305
518-388-4304

Schoharie County
157 Depot Lane
P.O. Box 689
Schoharie, New York 12157-0089
518-295-8114

Schuyler County
106 Tenth Street
Watkins Glen, New York 14891
607-535-8222

Seneca County
44 W. Williams Street
Waterloo, New York 13165
315-439-9241

Steuben County
Steuben County Jail
7007 Rumsey Street Ext.
Bath, New York 14810
607-776-7671

Sullivan County
County Jail
2 Bushnell Avenue
Monticello, New York 12701
845-794-7100

Tioga County
103 Corporate Drive
Owego, New York 13827
607-687-1010

Tompkins County
779 Warren Road
Ithaca, New York 14850
607-257-1345

Ulster County
129 Schwenk Drive
Kingston, New York 12401-2941
845-340-3802

Warren County
Warren County Municipal Center
1340 State Route 9
Lake George, New York 12845-9803
518-761-6477

Washington County
58 East Broadway
Salem, New York 12865
518-854-9245

Wayne County
7368 Route 31
Lyons, New York 14489-9107
315-946-9711 general number; 315-946-5793 civil process

Westchester County   www.westchestergov.com
1 Saw Mill River Parkway
Hawthorne, New York 10532
914-741-4400

Wyoming County   email: sheriff@wycol.com
151 North Main Street
Warsaw, New York 14569
585-786-8989

Yates County
Public Safety Building
227 Main Street
Penn Yan, New York 14527
315-536-5172

Chapter 10   Appeals

Most experts will agree that the appeal of a loss in the Small Claims Court is not worth the time or effort. The procedures are complicated and technical. This is why an experienced appellate attorney should be consulted if you intend to appeal the loss.

One of the better explanations of the general appellate process is contained in the Nassau County Small Claims Rules. Even though the rules are specific to Nassau County, the rules provide an understanding of the mechanics involved in the appellate process.

The Nassau County Rules (Appendix 2 at pages 15-16) specifically state:

> If you are dissatisfied with the judgment rendered in your case and believe that justice was not done, you may appeal from the judgment rendered by a judge (an arbitrator's award is not appealable). You may not appeal if you failed to appear for trial or upon any ground other than your assertion that substantial justice was not done in your case. The fact that you believe that there were technical defects of one kind or another in the trial will be of no assistance to you. The appellate court will consider the judgment reached only in the light of whether the trial judge rendered a just and fair decision.

> Before taking an appeal, there are some things you should know. The prosecution of an appeal requires a certain amount of legal skill which is probably a bit more than most laymen can muster.

If you lack that skill, you may need an attorney who will undoubtedly charge you a fee.

Another important requirement in taking an appeal is that you must purchase the minutes of the trial. This is a typewritten record of what has transpired at your trial. If the minutes were taken by a court reporter, contact the chief court reporter's office at (516) 572-2180, to obtain an estimate of the cost of the minutes. If a tape recorder was utilized for the case, correspond your request to the clerk of the Court for information regarding a transcription of the tape recorded hearing.

You should also bear in mind that the mere fact that you commence an appeal by the service and filing of a notice of appeal and paying the required fee does not stay your opponent from attempting to collect the judgment. To obtain a stay in connection with an appeal, the party who is appealing must file with the clerk of the Court an undertaking given by a surety in the amount of the judgment providing that if the judgment appealed from or any part of it is affirmed, or the appeal is dismissed, the appellant shall pay the amount directed to be paid by the judgment, or in lieu of filing an undertaking you may stay the collection of the judgment by depositing cash with the clerk in the amount of the judgment. The small claims "Notice of Appeal" forms are available at the clerk's office.

If you desire to represent yourself in the appeal, a notice of appeal must be served by someone, other than a party to the action, over the age of eighteen, by regular first class mail, upon your adversary within the thirty (30) day period and the original of said notice of appeal filed with the Court together with proof of service. There is a $25 fee for filing the notice of appeal.

Some people do prosecute their own appeals without counsel. It requires determination and skill. If you decide to appeal, you must do so within 30 days after judgment. Visit the clerk's office as soon after you receive notice of the results of your case. The clerk will advise you as to the initial step in taking the appeal but beyond that advice, the clerks are not equipped nor permitted to give legal advice.

*   *   *

Chapter 11
New York City Civil Court

If you are suing as a self-represented claimant in the New York City Civil Court, a copy of the Pro Se (a Latin expression meaning without an attorney) summons is annexed as FORM 10. You will need to hire a process server to serve the summons and complaint on the defendant if you are utilizing the Civil Court. Process servers are listed in various directories.

Some time ago, the New York City Civil Court released a one page document entitled Ten Tips From the Civil Clerk's Office. This document succinctly reflects the Court's perspective on common mistakes made by Civil Court litigants. Use these ideas as your own quality assurance check list:

1. Indicate court index number on all papers.

2. Characterize in the upper right portion of the first page the nature of the paper, e.g., "Affidavit in Opposition," "Order of Seizure."

3. File papers timely: don't trust the postal service! (Author's note: the creator of this document meant not to rely on the post office to timely deliver papers when there is a short deadline. Practice tip: file papers yourself or hire a filing service.)

4. When papers are mailed to the court, specify the part of the court they are directed to, e.g., landlord-tenant clerk, small claims department, civil judgment clerk, etc.

5. SIGN YOUR PAPER! (See Rule 130)

6.   Submit the proper fee. When in doubt, ask.

7. Trust deposit must be: cash; certified check or money order [not attorney check] Author's note: this refers to landlord-tenant matters.

8.   Check your calendar! Don't notice matters for court holidays.

9. When a response is expected from the clerk's office [e.g., copy of judgment, decision on motion etc.], always provide self-addressed envelope.

10. Be prompt for calendar call. It is NOT appropriate to stroll in for second call of the calendar.

(Author's note: the document bears no date.)

Chapter 12   Bankruptcy - the Debtor's Ultimate Trump Card

No discussion of the Small Claims Court System would be complete without a discussion about bankruptcy. The bankruptcy code was enacted by the U.S. Congress so its law supercedes any State or Local rule. That means that once a debtor formally files for bankruptcy protection, you must immediately comply with the bankruptcy rules regardless of your local court rules. Normally this means that you cannot proceed in small claims court litigation against the debtor and must bring your claim into the bankruptcy court. Since this area of the law is complex, I recommend that you seek the advice of an experienced attorney familiar with bankruptcy law.

Assuming you only have one small claim against one debtor, it is probably best to "transfer" your claim to the bankruptcy court, and see what happens. Generally this means filling out a Proof of Claim form if and only if the bankruptcy court instructs you to do so. In some cases, the debtor has so little assets that the Court tells you not to file a "proof of claim" form.

The purpose of bankruptcy court is to protect the debtor. Thus, in many circumstances, the debtor's debts are completely erased, known in legal jargon as "discharged," and those creditors with general unsecured claims (which are most creditors) receive little or nothing at all.

Unfortunately, this will be a reality you have to face when dealing with debtors. I remember an instance many years ago when I was a new attorney and a very important client called me with a very large debt collection. I was excited to be working on such a large case. I had all the invoices, all the proof I needed to win including signed contracts, and an admission by the defendant that the money was owed to my client. I served and filed the complaint and about two weeks later, I received a notice from the bankruptcy court that the debtor was seeking to dissolve its company. Since it had almost no marketable assets, my client was not able to recover any money because bankruptcy is the ultimate trump card. Moral of the story: be careful of who you lend credit to.

Practice Tip: If you are a debtor, it is always better to try to settle your debts if the overall amount of total debt is something you can reasonably pay off. Only use bankruptcy as a last resort. The law limits the number of times you can go bankrupt and not every debt can be erased. For example, no matter how bad your circumstances are, back taxes need to be paid. Always seek the advise of an experienced accountant and attorney before deciding to seek bankruptcy protection.

Chapter 13 Should I hire an attorney?

Now that you have had an overview of the small claims court system, you may be asking yourself the question "should I hire an attorney to take care of my case?" The purpose of this book is to empower the individual and the small business owner. The legal system can be ambiguous, confusing, and intimidating to anyone unfamiliar with the legal process or its unique jargon. Unfortunately, the legal system does everything possible to frustrate claimants because the Court system actively discourages the filing of claims whether these cases are small claims or class actions.

The Small Claims Court system achieves this negative goal by denying litigants the tools and the " real" information needed to navigate the legal system. It is my hope that this book provides the forms, information, tactics, and insight that will allow you to go to Court and use the system that your tax dollars created. After all, the small claims courts were designed to process small claims at a low cost to the claimant. Since you already pay for this system through your taxes (and Court fees), you might as well obtain the benefits of its function and also avoid the need to spend precious resources on the hiring of an attorney.

There will be times when it will be absolutely necessary to hire an attorney. The hiring of an attorney can range from a simple one hour office consultation to the creation of standard forms and contracts that will help you avoid litigation or enable you to sue debtors more successfully. It is your job to control legal costs by asking a number of pointed questions and exploring the cost effectiveness of each strategy. Make sure to also focus on ways to prevent your legal matter from recurring in the future.

Attorneys and the Need to Practice Preventive Medicine (and save on legal fees)

- In my law practice in New York, I have tried to practice "preventive medicine" by developing simple, custom forms for businesses to achieve effective uniformity and realistic vendor/client expectations. If you find that your business needs a few ounces of prevention, then make an appointment with an experienced attorney that you trust. If you need a recommendation, ask friends and colleagues who own businesses for a recommendation.

- Many times small business owners are reluctant to hire an attorney because of the expenses associated with legal representation. The best way to overcome this problem is to tell your attorney that you want a streamlined approach to resolving the legal issue. If one of your issues is debt collection, then try to determine the best way to collect the outstanding debt while reducing the need for litigation to collect future debts.

- In terms of debt collection, one successful method of prevention is to tighten your credit policy. Another is to know as much information about the businesses you are extending credit to. If you learn that a business has been sued for a number of different reasons, or has changed its name and address frequently, these are warning signs that you cannot ignore.

  There are a number of free resources you can advantage of in terms of running a background check on someone that you are to determine whether they are a credit risk. You can visit any of the local Courts and "run" the subject's name under the computerized defendant listings. (In New York, this would be in the Supreme Courts and the Civil Court Clerk's offices.) I am not aware of any small claims court computerized index systems in the New York City Small Claims Court system except in Manhattan.

There are also free web resources that you can experiment with. One site is "www.dos.state.ny.us" the official site of the New York State Department of Corporations. Check the corporation database for active and inactive corporations. If a corporation is listed as "inactive" you must not ignore this fact. **This is a warning sign not to lend credit**.

One common misperception by the general public is that the attorney can repair almost any situation. This is simply not true. If the facts or the law (or both) are against your position, minimize your loss. Sometimes it is best to mitigate (reduce) your damages -- which by the way is a legal obligation of all aggrieved parties--and move on.

Strategies to employ when Hiring an Attorney–tips for small business owners

You are a consumer and have the right to select and fire your vendors. This includes attorneys as well as other professionals. The reality is that you cannot conduct your small business without good legal and financial advice, but you should do everything to control legal costs and the amount of time devoted to legal issues. Clients who constantly resort to the legal system to resolve commercial disputes generally have issues that reach beyond the law that need to be looked at (e.g., sloppiness in record keeping, poor selection in employees that interface with the public).

Be mindful not to completely exclude your counsel from participating as a business advisor and certainly do not constantly haggle over every item in legal fees and expenses. A reasonable balance must be established and maintained. Lawyers are quite predictable. They tend to focus their attention on crises, and profitable endeavors. Thus, as a business client, I would recommend to small business owners to negotiate a fair and reasonable hourly rate or a flat fee. Lawyers who take on contingency fee work in the commercial context tend to ignore matters that do not settle quickly.

The New York State Bar Association has published a list of clients' rights and responsibilities which are included in the next section of this book. In order to reap the benefits of a healthy relationship with counsel, I suggest the following:

1. **Use different attorneys for different types of lawsuits. Since you would not ask a cardiologist to check on a knee disorder, the same advice applies to the legal profession.**

Make sure your attorney has the experience and resources (including the resource of time) to handle each project. Otherwise, obtain additional counsel for unique or complex matters.

2. **Have Clear and Concise Communications with Counsel.**

Communication failures are a major cause of lawyer-client disputes. Make sure that the goals of the project are clear, and the projected budget is realistically set and periodically reviewed. Always reconfirm meetings. Send detailed notes to counsel by fax or e-mail. The most inefficient message is "Mary called, please call back." A more effective message is, Mary express mailed the contract to Pennsylvania and will call you on Tuesday if the buyer agrees to the sale."

3. **Demand Monthly Invoices and Read Them Carefully.**

One mistake many busy lawyers make is not billing their clients monthly. All too often their time entries are cryptic because they are in a rush and timekeeping is generally regarded as a nuisance activity. In many ways, lawyers with late, cryptic time entries are doing themselves a great disservice because they generally devote a lot of time and effort to a project.

Examples:

> Inadequate Entry: Court appearance and related follow-up.....................................5 hours

> Better Entry: Court appearance at State Supreme Court before Justice X for preliminary scheduling conference. Meeting with adversary counsel before and after hearing. Call to expert regarding damage calculation. Drafted and served supplemental document demand (demand, back, affidavit of service). Travel time 45 minutes.................................5 hours

4.   **Pay your lawyer's bills on time**.

Lawyers treat clients who pay on time much better than all other clients. If you want prompt, effective service, pay promptly. Think about the people who owe your business money and what level of priority you give to them.

Anyone hiring an attorney in New York State is afforded certain rights and protections with respect to their representation by that attorney. In order to fully understand your rights, I have reproduced the listing of clients' rights as presented by the New York State Bar Association. **Internet Reference: http://courts.state.ny.us/clientrights2002.html**

This is the Statement of Client's Rights as Defined and Published by the New York State Bar Association.

This section directly quotes a document written and published by the New York State Bar Association. Please consult an attorney for any explanation of this document which should be posted in the lawyer's office if they are licensed to practice law in New York State. This document is included in this to empower individuals to work more effectively with their attorneys by being educated as to their rights.

Although this document was written for New York State licensed attorneys, its ideals are universal.

1. You are entitled to be treated with courtesy and consideration at all times by your lawyer and the other lawyers and personnel in your lawyer's office.

2. You are entitled to an attorney capable of handling your legal matter competently and diligently, in accordance with the highest standards of the profession. If you are not satisfied with how your matter is being handled, you have the right to withdraw from the attorney-client relationship at any time (court approval may be required in some matters and your attorney may have a claim against you for the value of services rendered to you up to the point of discharge).

3. You are entitled to your lawyer's independent professional judgment and

undivided loyalty uncompromised by conflicts of interest.

4. You are entitled to be charged a reasonable fee and to have your lawyer explain at the outset how the fee will be computed and the manner and frequency of billing. You are entitled to request and receive a written itemized bill from your attorney at reasonable intervals. You may refuse to enter into any fee arrangement that you find unsatisfactory. In the event of a fee dispute, you may have the right to seek arbitration; your attorney will provide you with the necessary information regarding arbitration in the event of a fee dispute, or upon your request.

5. You are entitled to have your questions and concerns addressed in a prompt manner and to have your telephone calls returned promptly.

6. You are entitled to be kept informed as to the status of your matter and to request and receive copies of papers. You are entitled to sufficient information to allow you to participate meaningfully in the development of your matter.

7. You are entitled to have your legitimate objectives respected by your attorney; including whether or not to settle your matter (court approval of a settlement is required in some matters).

8. You have the right to privacy in your dealings with your lawyer and to have your

secrets and confidences preserved to the extent permitted by law.

9. You are entitled to have your attorney conduct himself or herself ethically in accordance with the Code of Professional Responsibility.

10. You may not be refused representation on the basis of race, creed, color, religion, sex, sexual orientation, age, national origin or disability.

While clients have rights, they also have certain responsibilities. These responsibilities are listed below:

This is the Statement of Client's Responsibilities as Defined and Published by the New York Bar. For any questions please contact the New York State Bar Association.

Reciprocal trust, courtesy and respect are the hallmarks of the attorney-client relationship. Within that relationship, the client looks to the attorney for expertise, education, sound judgment, protection, advocacy and representation. These expectations can be achieved only if the client fulfills the following responsibilities:

1. The client is expected to treat the lawyer and the lawyer's staff with courtesy and consideration.

2. The client's relationship with the lawyer must be one of complete candor and the lawyer must be apprised of all facts or circumstances of the matter being handled by the lawyer even if the client believes that those facts may be detrimental to the client's cause or unflattering to the client.

3. The client must honor the fee arrangement as agreed to with the lawyer, in accordance with law.

4. All bills for services rendered which are tendered to the client pursuant to the agreed upon fee arrangement should be paid promptly.

5. The client may withdraw from the attorney-client relationship, subject to

financial commitments under the agreed to fee arrangement, and, in certain circumstances, subject to court approval.

6. Although the client should expect that his or her correspondence, telephone calls and other communications will be answered within a reasonable time frame, the client should recognize that the lawyer has other clients equally demanding of the lawyer's time and attention.

7. The client should maintain contact with the lawyer, promptly notify the lawyer of any change in telephone number or address and respond promptly to a request by the lawyer for information and cooperation.

8. The client must realize that the lawyer need respect only legitimate objectives of the client and that the lawyer will not advocate or propose positions which are unprofessional or contrary to law or the Lawyer's Code of Professional Responsibility.

9. The lawyer may be unable to accept a case if the lawyer has previous professional commitments which will result in inadequate time being available for the proper representation of a new client.

10.   A lawyer is under no obligation to accept a client if the lawyer determines that the cause of the client is without merit, a conflict of interest would exist or that a suitable working relationship with the client is not likely.

Conclusion

Our system of justice depends on the vigilance of all individuals to enforce their rights. This book provides the knowledge and forms needed to file your case and understand the procedures and jargon used in the Court system.

I wish you luck in your endeavors. I hope to prepare a second edition of this book, and to that effect, I ask that you send your comments and suggestions by post card to P.O. Box 604173, Bayside, New York 11360-4173.

To find out more about the New York State Legal system, please visit the official site: www.courts.state.ny.us

Good luck!

Special Thanks

I would like to thank the following individuals for all of their help in the creation of this book and its related internet sites:

Cynthia Jameson
Alex Ubieta: website and cover design
Jill Lam
Tekks Grafix, New York City
Dr. Seymour Meyer, M.D., F.A.C.S., D-S
William D. Paness, C.M.A., M.B.A.
Mike Vooss
David I. Perry, D.S.W.
DCNet2000.com

and all the clients who asked me to file small claims cases on their behalf especially Maria C. Scarano.

This book is the result of many years of study, research, and experience (or as my parents would say, the "school of hard knocks"). Thus, I also wish to express my deep admiration for Michelle Sufrin, whose dedication to the education of tomorrow's leaders is inspirational. She is an example of the excellent teachers who encouraged me and shared their wisdom and vision with me when I was a student. I hope that this book shares some of the wisdom that I have acquired over the past with my readers.

Special thanks to Marty Porush, Mike Golub, Moises and Mary Faidengold, Hunter McGeary, and Rob Minster for being great friends throughout the years.

Finally, the most important thanks are extended to Ken Pyburn and Michael Ponterio, Esq. who, in action, demonstrate true friendship, integrity, and loyalty.

The forms contained in this book
are scanned images and are
included for your reference.

Please obtain current copies of
these forms from the appropriate
Clerk's office where applicable.

Appendix 1

A GUIDE FOR THE
USE OF THE
COMMERCIAL CLAIMS PART

New York State
Unified Court System

Judith S. Kaye Chief Judge	**Jonathan Lippman** Chief Administrative Judge

(Effective September, 1996)

TABLE OF CONTENTS

WHAT IS THE COMMERCIAL CLAIMS COURT?

The Commercial Claims Court is an informal court where corporations, partnerships and associations can sue for money only, up to $3,000, without a lawyer.

For example, if you feel that a person or business damaged something of yours, you may sue that person or business for the monetary amount of your damages. You also may sue a person or business for money damages arising out of a dispute over a contract. You cannot, however, in Commercial Claims Court, compel that person or business to fix the damaged item or require the performance of the act promised in the advertisement. Your lawsuit can be only for money.

Most Commercial Claims Courts have a clerk who can assist you with the procedures for bringing your lawsuit. When this booklet mentions the clerk, and the court you are using does not have a clerk, you should seek the assistance of the judge.

WHO CAN USE THE COMMERCIAL CLAIMS COURT?

Any corporation, including a municipal corporation or public benefit corporation, partnership, or association, which has its principal office in the State of New York, or an assignee of any commercial claim[1], may file a claim. A corporation, partnership, or association may not bring more than five commercial claims actions or proceedings per calendar month anywhere in the State.

If you sue in Commercial Claims Court, you are the claimant (plaintiff); if you have been sued, you are the defendant. You can sue more than one defendant in the same case if necessary.

If you are sued, and you believe that a third party is responsible for the claim, you may be able to bring that party into the lawsuit as a defendant. Contact the clerk of the Commercial Claims Court for information about a "third-party action."

If you choose, you may be represented by an attorney at your own expense. In addition to being represented by an attorney, a partnership may be represented by any one of the partners, and a corporation may be represented by any authorized officer, director, or employee of the corporation provided that the representative has the authority to settle the case or to conduct the trial on behalf of the corporation. If there are attorneys on both sides, the case may be transferred to a regular part of the court.

WHERE ARE THE COMMERCIAL CLAIMS COURTS LOCATED?

Commercial Claims Courts are located in the New York City Civil Court (beginning 1/1/91), in all City Courts, and in the District Courts in Nassau

---

[1]Collection agencies, or entities that take assignments of debts for the purpose of bringing an action in the Commercial Claims Court, may not use the Commercial Claims Court.

1

and Suffolk Counties. Consult your telephone book for the address and phone number of your local court and call that local court for information.

HOW DO I START A COMMERCIAL CLAIMS CASE?

You, or someone on your behalf, must come to the Commercial Claims Court to file a statement of your claim.

You should be prepared to give a brief written statement of the facts that form the basis of your claim. Check any documents relating to your case for the relevant dates and names. If you are suing on a contract or for property damage, you may claim interest as well as money damages.

If you are suing on a claim based on a consumer transaction — one where the money, property or service which is the subject of the transaction is primarily for personal, family or household purposes — you must send a demand letter to the defendant at least 10 and no more than 180 days before you start the lawsuit. You can get a demand letter form from the clerk of the court.

You must sue in a court having a Commercial Claims Court in a county or district where the defendant lives or works or has a place of business.

You will be required to pay a filing fee of $20 plus the cost of mailing a notice of the claim to the defendant. You will also be required to file a verification that no more than five (5) commercial claims have been instituted by you anywhere in the State during the calendar month. In a claim based on a consumer transaction, you also will have to certify that you sent a demand letter.

When the claim is filed, the clerk will tell the claimant when the case will be tried. The clerk will then send the notice of claim to the defendant by both certified mail and ordinary first class mail. The notice of claim tells the defendant when the case will be tried and gives a brief statement of your claim and the amount of money you are seeking. If the copy of the claim sent by ordinary mail is not returned as undeliverable within 21 days (30 days for a claim based on a consumer transaction), the defendant is presumed to have received notice even if the claim sent by certified mail has not been delivered.

If the notice is not delivered by the post office, the court will set a new trial date and tell the claimant how to arrange for personal service of the notice of claim on the defendant. Personal service may be made by any person (including a friend or a relative) who is 18 years of age or older, except that you or any other party to the action may not serve the notice of claim.

If service of the notice cannot be made upon the defendant within four months of the date when the action was first started, the action will be dismissed without prejudice to your bringing the action at a later time.

A Commercial Claims case will not proceed to trial until the defendant has been served with a notice of claim.

MUST I KNOW THE DEFENDANT'S CORRECT NAME?

When filing a Commercial Claims case, the claimant must provide the name and address of the person or business being sued. If you do not know the correct legal name of the defendant, you can sue using any name under which the defendant does business. However, you should go to the office of the County Clerk in the county where the business is located to find out who owns the business and the legal name of the business. The County Clerk's office keeps a record of the names under which businesses are operated.

If you discover the defendant's correct "legal" name before the trial date, return to the Commercial Claims Court and have the case papers changed to state the correct name of the defendant.

WHAT IS A COUNTERCLAIM?

Sometimes the defendant may have a claim against the claimant and may countersue the claimant in the same case. This is known as a "counterclaim," and it can be made for up to $3,000 in money damages. The defendant must come to court prepared to prove the counterclaim and should make the counterclaim known to the judge or arbitrator on the date of the trial. The judge then may either proceed with the trial or adjourn it for a short period of time. If you receive notice of a counterclaim against you, contact the Commercial Claims Court to see what procedures you should follow. Be prepared to try both your own case and the counterclaim at the time of the trial.

Any counterclaim for more than $3,000 cannot be brought to a Commercial Claims Court; it must be brought in another part of the court or in another court.

ADJOURNMENTS

Adjournments in Commercial Claims Court are discouraged. Only the judge can grant an adjournment. However, either party may request the hearing be rescheduled in the evening, provided that such evening hours do not cause unreasonable hardship to either party. If you are the defendant, you must request an evening hearing within 14 days of receipt of the notice of claim.

If you are going to ask for an adjournment, notify the other party in advance. Either you or someone on your behalf should appear in court to explain to the judge why you cannot be ready for trial. Some courts permit adjournments to be requested by mail or by telephone (adjournments by telephone are not available in New York City and in Nassau and Suffolk Counties), and you should contact the court to find out the method of adjournment. If you do not have a good excuse, your request may be denied and, if you are not ready to go to trial, your case may be dismissed, or if you are the defendant, an award may be made against you without your having been heard.

WHAT SHOULD I DO AT TRIAL?

On the date set for trial, you should arrive at the court before the calendar of cases is called. Contact the Commercial Claims Court to find out the hour at which court begins. If the claimant is late, the case may be dismissed.

If the defendant is late, a default judgment against the defendant may be granted.

When you arrive, check the Commercial Claims calendar posted on the wall outside the courtroom, or with the clerk if there is no calendar posted, to see that your case is scheduled.

When the clerk calls your case, stand and state your name and tell the court that you are ready to proceed with your case. If you are requesting an adjournment, tell the clerk at that time. The trial is a simple, informal hearing before a judge or arbitrator.

SHOULD I CHOOSE A JUDGE OR AN ARBITRATOR?

In many courts, only judges are available to try cases. However, in New York City, Nassau and Westchester Counties, the cities of Buffalo and Rochester and some other locations, both judges and arbitrators are available to try cases.

An arbitrator is an experienced lawyer·who serves without pay. Where arbitrators are used, there usually are many arbitrators available and only one or two judges. Your case can be tried by an arbitrator if both sides agree. If you and the defendant agree to have your case heard by an arbitrator, the case probably will be heard sooner because there are more arbitrators than judges.

Do not hesitate to have your case tried by an arbitrator. He or she will apply the same law to your case as the judge would apply. The hearing before an arbitrator is less formal, and you may not be as nervous as you might be before a judge. When an arbitrator determines a case, the decision is final, so that there is no further appeal by either the claimant or defendant.

ARE THERE ANY JURY TRIALS?

The claimant in a Commercial Claims action cannot demand a jury trial. A defendant, however, may demand a trial by jury. If a defendant demands a jury trial, the defendant must pay a jury fee and file a $50.00 "undertaking" (security) with the court to guarantee the payment of costs that may be awarded against the defendant. The defendant also is required to make an affidavit specifying the issues of fact which the defendant desires to have tried by a jury, and stating that such trial is desired and demanded in good faith. The Commercial Claims Clerk will answer your questions regarding the procedures for obtaining a jury trial. Jury trials are held before panels of six jurors.

PREPARING FOR TRIAL

1. Evidence

Before trial, you should gather all the evidence necessary to prove your claim or your defense. Anything that will help prove the facts in dispute should be brought to court. This includes photographs, written agreements, an itemized bill or invoice that is receipted or marked "paid," written estimates of the cost of service or repairs, a receipt for the purchase of an item or the payment, of a debt, cancelled checks, and correspondence. If you rely on estimates, two different written itemized estimates of the cost of repairs or services are required. If possible, merchandise that is in dispute should be brought to court.

Testimony, including your own, is evidence. Any legally competent witness whose testimony is important to your case may testify. This can be a person who witnessed your transaction or someone whose special knowledge and experience makes him or her an expert on the cost of the services or repairs that were provided or may be required.

You may have to pay an expert witness for his or her time.

2. Subpoenas

If you are unable to get a witness to appear voluntarily, you may apply for issuance of a subpoena to the clerk of the Commercial Claims Court, who will give you the necessary information.

A subpoena is a legal document that commands the person named in the subpoena to appear in court. An expert witness may not be compelled to testify by subpoena, but you may pay the expert witness for coming to court to testify.

You also may apply to the clerk of the Commercial Claims Court for a ''subpoena duces tecum,'' which is a legal document that directs someone to produce a bill, receipt, or other written document or record you need.

Either party may apply for a subpoena up to 48 hours before the trial date.

You may arrange for service of the subpoena and the payment of a $15.00 witness fee and, where appropriate, travel expenses for the person subpoenaed. Except where the travel is entirely within a city, a subpoenaed witness is entitled to 23 cents a mile as travel expense to and from the court from the place he or she was served with the subpoena. Service of the subpoena may be done by any person (including a friend or relative) who is 18 years of age or older, except that you or any other party to the action may not serve the subpoena.

HOW IS A TRIAL CONDUCTED?

The claimant's case is presented first. After being sworn as a witness, the claimant will tell his or her version of the incident. All papers or other evidence should be shown at this time. When the claimant has finished testifying, the judge or arbitrator or the defendant may ask some questions to clarify matters. The claimant may present other witnesses in support of the claimant, and they, too, may be questioned by the judge or arbitrator or the defendant.

The defendant will then be sworn and tell his or her side of the story and present evidence. The defendant also may present other witnesses. The claimant or the judge or arbitrator may ask questions of the defendant and the witnesses called by the defendant.

If you are suing a business, be certain to ask the defendant's witness the full and correct legal name of the business and the name of the person who owns the business. If the name of the business is different from the name you wrote in your notice of claim, ask the judge or arbitrator to make any correction in the name on your notice of claim.

After all the evidence is presented, the judge or arbitrator will consider the evidence and render a decision. The decision will be mailed to the parties within a few days after the hearing. In rare cases, the decision may be announced immediately after the trial.

WHAT HAPPENS IF ONE PARTY DOES NOT APPEAR?

If the claimant does not appear in court when the calendar is called, the case will be dismissed.

If the defendant does not appear, the court will direct an 'inquest'' (hearing). That means that the claimant will go before the judge or arbitrator to present evidence to prove his or her case without the defendant presenting any evidence. If the claimant's case is proved, a "default" judgment will be awarded against the defendant.

If a default judgment is granted because the defendant did not appear, or the case is dismissed because the claimant did not appear, the losing party may ask the court to re-open the case and restore it for a trial upon a showing of good cause. Contact the clerk for the procedure used to re-open the case. The clerk also will set a date when both sides are to return to court.

On the return date, the judge will decide whether to re-open the case. However, both sides should be prepared for trial in the event the case is re-opened.

SETTLEMENTS

In a lawsuit, one of the parties must always lose. Although you believe you are entitled to win, the judge or arbitrator may rule against you. Therefore, parties to a commercial claims action are encouraged to settle their cases whenever possible. You should seriously consider a reasonable offer of settlement.

If the case is settled before the day of trial and the money has been paid, notify the clerk by mail. You do not have to appear in court.

If a case is settled but the money has not been paid, or if settlement talks are not completed, the claimant should appear in court so that the case is not dismissed and ask the judge for "adjournment pending settlement." A new date then will be set for trial. If the settlement does not work out, both parties should appear in court on the new adjourned date, prepared for trial.

CAN I APPEAL THE CASE IF I LOSE?

If your case was tried by a judge, you may appeal the decision if you believe justice was not done. You cannot appeal if your case was tried by an arbitrator.

Technical mistakes made during the trial are not grounds for reversal. The appellate court will consider only whether substantial justice was done.

Very few Commercial Claims cases are appealed. The expense of appealing is rarely justified in a Commercial Claims action. Taking an appeal may require retaining an attorney. In addition, the party who is appealing must purchase a typed transcript of the trial proceedings from the court reporter, or from the court when audio recording of the trial is authorized. If no stenographic minutes were taken, the party appealing will be required to prepare a statement of what took place during the proceeding, or in some courts, the judge or clerk will write this statement. If a statement is used, the party who is not appealing will have an opportunity to offer changes to the statement.

If you decide to appeal, you must file a notice of appeal and pay the required fee within 30 days after the judgment is entered. Consult the Commercial Claims clerk if you want further information about starting an appeal.

The party appealing the judgment can temporarily prevent its enforcement pending the decision on the appeal. To do this, a bond or undertaking must be filed with the court to guarantee payment of the judgment should the party lose the appeal. If you receive a notice of appeal, you should call the court to find out if an undertaking has been posted; if not, you may take steps necessary to collect the judgment immediately, or you may wait until the appeal has been decided.

WHAT DO I DO IF I WIN?

If the claimant wins, the court will enter a judgment for a sum of money. The court also may require the claimant to take certain action - for example, return damaged merchandise to the defendant - before entering judgment.

HOW CAN I COLLECT MY JUDGMENT?

Winning a judgment does not guarantee you will collect.

The court provides some help in collection of judgments. For example, prior to rendering judgment, the court can order the defendant to disclose his or her assets and restrain the defendant from disposing of them. However, you must take the necessary steps to obtain payment of your judgment.

After winning a judgment in your favor, you should try to contact the losing party to collect your judgment. If the defendant does not pay you, you may need the services of an enforcement officer - a sheriff, city marshal, or a constable. You must provide that office with the information needed to locate assets (money or property) of the defendant, and the enforcement officer then can seize those assets to satisfy your judgment. The enforcement officer may request mileage and other fees before he or she seizes the assets. In many circumstances, these fees later can be added to the original judgment amount you receive from the defendant.

Property which may be reached by an enforcement officer includes: bank accounts, wages, houses or other real estate, automobiles, stocks and bonds.

LOCATING ASSETS

1. Information Subpoenas

If a Commercial Claims judgment has been entered in your favor you may obtain an information subpoena or subpoenas from the Commercial Claims clerk upon payment of a $2.00 fee. If you request it, the clerk will assist you in the preparation and use of the information subpoena forms. Some stationery stores also sell information subpoena forms.

An information subpoena is a legal document that may help you to discover the location of assets of the judgment debtor (defendant). It is a legal direction to a person or institution to answer certain questions about where the assets of the defendant are located. The information subpoena may be served upon the judgment debtor and upon any person or corporation that you believe has knowledge of the judgment debtor's assets - for example, the telephone company, landlord, or bank. Separate forms are used for service on the judgment debtor and service on any other person or corporation.

The person or corporation served with an information subpoena must answer the questions served with the subpoena within seven days of receipt.

The information subpoena, accompanied by two copies of a set of written questions, and a prepaid addressed return envelope, may be served by ordinary mail or by certified mail, return receipt requested. Except where service is to be made upon the judgment debtor, a fee of 50 cents also must accompany the subpoena.

2. Bank Accounts and Wages

One simple way to improve the chances of collecting your judgment is to learn the name and address of the bank where the defendant keeps a savings or checking account. A way to do this is to look at the back of a cancelled check you or a friend may have given to the defendant. With this information, the enforcement officer can seize money in the defendant's account and use the funds to satisfy your judgment.

Another way is to find out the name and address of the defendant's employer. If you sued an employed person, you may be able to collect your judgment out of his or her salary. To do this, the enforcement officer can serve an "income execution" on the employer of the judgment debtor. This execution requires the debtor's employer to pay 10% of the judgment debtor's salary to you until the judgment is paid, provided the debtor's gross earnings are above a certain minimum amount set by federal law (currently $127.00 per week).

8

3. Real Property

If defendant owns real property in the county, you may be able to collect your judgment from its sale. The clerk will direct you to the proper office where you can check property ownership. You will have to obtain a transcript of your Commercial Claims judgment from the court and file it with the County Clerk. You then should consult the sheriff, who may conduct a sale at public auction. It is your responsibility to prepare the papers required to sell the property. The sheriff, after deducting his or her fees and expenses, and, after paying off any prior mortgage, tax liens, and judgments, will send the balance to you up to the amount of your judgment, plus interest.

4. Personal Property

Your judgment can be paid from the sale of defendant's personal property, such as automobiles, stocks and bonds and equipment. Contact the enforcement officer for details of the expenses and fees required. It is your responsibility to prepare the papers required to sell the property.

If you give an enforcement officer the model, year, and license plate number as well as the location of the defendant's automobile, the officer can seize it, sell it at auction and pay your judgment with the proceeds. You can check with the New York State Department of Motor Vehicles to learn whether defendant owns an automobile (Fill out form FS-25). You can also find out from the Department of Motor Vehicles (Form MV-905) whether a bank or finance company already has a claim against defendant's car.

If the defendant has a large unpaid auto loan, a bank or finance company might be entitled to payment of the loan from the sale of the defendant's vehicle before your judgment can be satisfied.

OTHER ENFORCEMENT PROCEDURES

1. Claims Based on Motor Vehicle Ownership

If your claim was based on the defendant's ownership or operation of a motor vehicle, you may be able to have the Department of Motor Vehicles suspend the defendant's drivers license and auto registration until the judgment is paid. To take advantage of this procedure, you must have a judgment for over $600 which has remained unpaid more than 15 days after it becomes final. Ask the clerk for details of this procedure.

2. Licensing Agencies

If the judgment debtor is engaged in a business that is licensed or certified, you may notify the appropriate state or local authority if the judgment remains unpaid 35 days after the judgment debtor receives notice of entry of the judgment. The failure to pay a judgment may be considered by the licensing authority as a basis for the revoking, suspending, or refusing to grant or renew a license to operate a business.

If the judgment debtor is a business that the court finds to be engaged in fraudulent or illegal conduct, you have the right to notify the Attorney General and, if the business if licensed, the appropriate licensing authority as well.

Appendix 2

WHAT IS A SMALL CLAIM?

If you have a claim against any person or business firm for which you believe that you are entitled to a sum of money not exceeding $3000, and the person you wish to sue either resides, is employed or has a place of business in Nassau County, or the business firm is located in Nassau, then such a cause of action is a small claim and you may sue the defendant in one of the District Courts of Nassau County.

The following are some examples of the more common kinds of actions instituted in small claims:

Claims against,

Appliance repair companies for shoddy work, or for failure to perform as agreed.

Garage mechanics and home improvement firms where you believe you have been cheated.

Clients, patients and customers for the cost of services rendered to them by you.

Business firms for the return of cash deposits or to recover damages for breach of contract.

Employers for wages due,

Persons or companies for the price of goods sold to them by you.

Persons or firms that have negligently damaged your property or caused you to suffer personal injuries,

Dry cleaning firms and laundries for damage caused by them to your clothing, drapes, etc.

Business firms or other persons for the loss or conversion of your property.

4

Persons for injuries sustained by you because of an assault.

The above list is by no means complete. You may have a claim under many other circumstances where you or your property have been harmed and you desire financial redress for the wrong. One important fact to bear in mind is that the only relief afforded a plaintiff in small claims is the recovery of money. If, for example, someone or some business firm has wrongfully withheld your property, you cannot sue the defendant in small claims to recover the property although you may sue in small claims for the value of the property providing it is valued at $3000 or less. So too, you cannot bring a small claims suit to compel someone to do something nor to prevent someone from committing some harm to you or your property. The only result that can be achieved in small claims is the recovery of money.

DO YOU NEED A LAWYER TO START
A SMALL CLAIMS SUIT?

No. It is not necessary for you to hire an attorney to start a small claims action. The procedure is not complicated and if you follow the instructions in this pamphlet and any other information court personnel may give you after the suit has begun, you will not encounter too much difficulty. The trial of a small claims case is simple and informal and no particular legal expertise is necessary for you to present your case in court. More will be said about the conduct of a small claims trial later in the pamphlet.

The foregoing does not mean that you cannot be represented by a lawyer in small claims. If you desire to have an attorney, you certainly are permitted to retain one.

DO YOU NEED A LAWYER IF YOU
ARE SUED IN SMALL CLAIMS?

Individuals who are sued in small claims are not required to hire counsel although they may do so if they wish.

HOW MUCH DOES IT COST TO START
A SMALL CLAIMS SUIT?

At the time you commence your small claims case you will have to pay a $10.00filing fee if your claim is for $1.000, or less. The fee is $15 where your claim exceeds $1.000. No personal or business checks are accepted as payment.

WHO MAY BRING A SMALL CLAIMS SUIT?

Any person, including those under eighteen years of age as well as partnerships and associations, may sue in small claims. It is not required that you live or work in Nassau in order to avail yourself of the privilege of bringing a small claims action. Business corporations, insurance companies and assignees of claims, may not sue in small claims, although they may be sued.

Similar in nature to Small Claims, Commercial Claims actions are available for small corporations to institute a claim up to $3000. Contact the Clerk of the Small Claims Court for specific applicabilities, limitations and fees. The booklet "A Guide to Commercial Claims" is also available.

If you are under eighteen years of age, one of your parents having custody, or if you have no parents, the person in whose custody you reside, must appear for you in the case. If you are under eighteen and married to an adult, your spouse may appear. This simply means that at the time you wish to start your small claims suit you must be accompanied to court by the person who will appear for you. That person's signature will be necessary to start the action. In addition, that person will have to be with you in court on the day of the trial.

LOCATION OF THE DISTRICT COURTS
THAT HANDLE SMALL CLAIMS

Small Claims cases are tried in three District Court Locations. Small Claims cases are not, however, heard everyday in every court. You may telephone the courts listed below to find out the days of the week Small Claims are on the calendar.

Daytime Small Claims Parts   (At: 9:30 A. M.)

Hempstead Part – 2nd District – Civil Clerks Office
99 Main Street, Hempstead, New York 11550
Telephone 572-2262

Great Neck Part – 3rd District
435 Middle Neck Road, Great Neck, New York   11023
Telephone 571-8400

Hicksville Part –4th District
87 Bethpage Road, Hicksville, New York 11801
Telephone 571-7090

If you wish to have your case heard in the daytime, you may file your claim in one of the three courts listed above. There is no limitation with respect to the selection of the court. Many plaintiffs choose to file in a court which is convenient to their home.

Night Small Claims:

Civil Part – 1st District
99 Main Street, Hempstead, New York 11550
Telephone 572-2262

You may initiate a night small claim at the Great Neck Part, Hicksville Part or the 1st District Part during normal business hours. The evening session is only conducted at 99 Main Street, Hempstead, New York, at : 6:00 p.m.

HOW TO START A SMALL CLAIMS ACTION

You must personally visit the court to start the action. The civil cashier is open from 9 a.m. to 4:30 p.m. any weekday, except legal holidays. The initial step in small claims requires a personal visit to the court. This particular task cannot be accomplished by mail nor on the telephone.

If you are unable to come to court to start the suit, it may be commenced by someone acting in your behalf. When you arrive at court

7

you or the person acting for you will be required to complete a form which calls for the inclusion of your name and address, the name and street address of the person or firm you wish to sue and a brief statement of the facts of your claim against the defendant. You will also have to state the amount of money you seek as damages. When the form has been completed you or the person acting for you will be required to sign the form.

If you are under eighteen years of age, one of the persons mentioned under the section "WHO MAY BRING A SMALL CLAIMS SUIT" will have to accompany you to court to sign the complaint form.

Upon the occasion of your visit to the court, you will be required to pay the filing fee mentioned earlier in the pamphlet.

The clerk will inform you of the date & time set for your trial and will give you a printed form which will serve as a reminder to you of the trial date. The clerk will also prepare a summons that will be sent by the court by certified mail, return receipt requested to the defendant at the address supplied by you. If the defendant does not reside in Nassau County but works in Nassau the summons will be mailed to the individuals place of employment. If you wish to sue more than one defendant in the same action, a summons will be mailed to each. The summons will also be sent by regular mail.

WHAT YOU MUST DO IF THE POST OFFICE IS UNABLE TO DELIVER THE SUMMONS TO THE DEFENDANT

If after your visit to the court you hear nothing further, you may safely assume that the post office has delivered the summons and your case is ready for trial. In some cases, however, the post office is unable to effect delivery either because the defendant has moved or the address supplied by you is incorrect or for some other reason. If this should happen in your case, you will be promptly notified by the court. If you wish to continue the suit, it will then be necessary for you to arrange to have the summons personally served upon the defendant.

Under these circumstances the court will give you a new trial date at a time later than the original date and will mail the summons, an instruction form and an affidavit of service to you. The instruction form sets forth in detail how and by whom a summons may be served. The summons must be served upon the defendant in Nassau County by someone 18 years of age or older other than yourself. After it has been served, the person who served the summons must complete the affidavit of service and sign it before a notary public. As soon as this has been done, you should mail the completed affidavit of service to the court. Upon receipt of the affidavit, the court will place your case upon the trial calendar on the new trial date. If you have been unable to effect service of the summons, you should notify the court so that you may be given more time to accomplish service. A small claims case cannot proceed to trial until the defendant has been served with the summons.

WHAT YOU SHOULD DO IF YOU ARE SUED IN SMALL CLAIMS

If you wish to defend yourself, make certain that you appear at the proper time and place. If you ignore the summons, or forget to come to court, it will probably be too late afterwards to do anything about it for in all likelihood the plaintiff will have a default judgment against you on the day of trial. It is possible to have a default judgment vacated, however it requires more legal knowledge to accomplish this than this pamphlet can impart. Should this happen to you and it should be avoided at all costs, you may require the services of an attorney to attempt to vacate the judgment.

Sometimes it occurs that a person who is sued in small claims has a claim against the person who is suing him or her. This is known as a counterclaim. If this is the situation in your case you should visit the court where the trial is scheduled within five (5) days of receipt of the summons. You will complete a form at the clerk's office entitled "Statement of Counterclaim". The fee is $3 plus the cost of postage to send your counterclaim by first class mail to the claimant. If you fail to file a counterclaim until the time of the hearing (orally to the judge at the time the case is called in the courtroom), the claimant may request and obtain an adjournment of the hearing to a later date so that he can prepare to defend against the counterclaim. You cannot counterclaim for more than $3,000. If you have a claim against the plaintiff for more than $3,000 and you wish to sue him or her you will have to bring a separate suit in the civil part of the court.

MAY YOU HAVE A JURY TRIAL?

Ordinarily there are no jury trials in small claims, the cases being heard before a judge without a jury. The person who starts the action in small claims waives the right to trial before a jury.

The situation is different for the defendant. If the defendant desires a jury trial, he or she can obtain one providing they file with the court a demand for a trial by jury together with an affidavit setting forth that there are issues of fact in the case requiring a jury trial and specifying what those issues are and containing a statement that the jury trial is desired and intended in good faith. This must be done prior to the day of trial and at the same time the defendant will be required to pay a jury fee of $55.00 to the clerk, and an undertaking in the sum of $50.00 cash or bond.

The foregoing instructions apply only if the defendant desires a jury trial. Failing to comply with the instructions, the trial will take place before a judge without a jury.

WHAT YOU SHOULD DO TO
PREPARE FOR TRIAL

Probably the most important part of a lawsuit is the preparation that goes into it. How well you prepare your suit or defense will have a considerable impact on the result of the trial. Many lawsuits are lost simply because of a failure to subpoena an important witness or to introduce a particular document or record.

The first thing you should do is to analyze your claim. It will be necessary for you to prove each element of your case at the trial. some parts of the case can be established by your own testimony, other parts by the testimony of other people who are called witnesses. Still other parts can be proven by the records and documents.

An example of what is meant might be helpful. Let us assume that you are suing a store to recover a deposit of one hundred dollars given by you as a down payment on an article of furniture you intended to buy. At the time of the transaction, the salesperson told you that the furniture would be delivered in two weeks whereupon you gave him $100 in cash and received a sales slip acknowledging the receipt of the money. After several weeks, the furniture had not been delivered nor have you been able to get your deposit back.

Your testimony as to what transpired is essential. In addition, it would be important for you to bring the sales slip to the trial and to introduce it in evidence. If you have given a check for the deposit rather than cash, your canceled check would be an important piece of evidence to introduce.

Suppose for example, you are a defendant in a small claims case where one of your neighbors is suing you for $500 claiming that you assaulted him or her and caused personal injuries. Let us assume that in actual fact you did have an argument with the neighbor but no blows were struck and neither of you was harmed. If at the time there were other persons present that you are able to identify, it would be essential to your case as defendant to subpoena one or more of those persons as a witness or witnesses in your behalf. If your spouse, a neighbor and the local mail carrier were present when the event took place, it would be the better course to subpoena the mail carrier and the neighbor as witnesses rather than call your spouse. While relatives may testify, and should be called when there are no other witnesses available, judges are inclined to be more impressed with the testimony of persons unrelated to a party.

One more point to remember is that a letter or statement of a witness, even if the witness has signed the document before a notary public, cannot be used in court as evidence. The witness must appear personally and testify.

Give your case a lot of thought - prepare - if you want to subpoena witnesses the next part of the pamphlet tells you how to do it.

WITNESSES – HOW TO GET THEM TO COURT

In some cases the person you desire to have as a witness will come willingly to court. Under those circumstances, simply tell the person when and where you want him or her to appear. If your prospective witness will not or cannot appear voluntarily, you should visit the court where the trial is scheduled and request the form entitled "Application for Subpoena". Please note that a subpoena cannot be issued until the defendant has been served the summons. This may be determined by calling the clerk's office. You should file the "Application for Subpoena" form at least ten (10) days before your trial date, as it takes several days for the clerk's office to process your application and prepare the subpoena. There is no charge for this service. The subpoena with instructions for its service will be mailed to you. The court does not serve subpoenas. Please be advised that the person who serves the subpoena will have to pay the witness a $15 fee plus round-trip mileage of 23 cents per mile.

Our final word regarding subpoenas. The court cannot subpoena your own "expert" (i. e. mechanic or medical provider). You may very well have to pay your "expert" whatever he requests for his time to appear and testify in your behalf.

PROOF OF DAMAGES

There are many cases where a person brings suit in the small claims court to recover money for damage done to his or her property. The most familiar example of this is the automobile accident case where one party sues another for damage to the plaintiff's automobile as a result of a collision.

One of the things that the plaintiff must prove to win the case is the amount of damage sustained by the automobile as a result of the accident. There are several ways that this can be done. If the plaintiff has had the automobile repaired, he or she should bring to court with them the itemized bill or invoice receipted or marked, "paid". If the plaintiff has not had the car repaired, he or she should bring two itemized estimates describing the damage and the cost of repair. In either case, these documents are admissible in evidence and are proof of the reasonable value and the necessity of the repairs. If the plaintiff prefers, he or she may bring an expert witness who has inspected the automobile for the purpose of testifying as to the damages and the cost of the repair.

These rules apply as well to cases involving the damage to other property and are not limited solely to the automobile accident case.

A final word concerning the automobile collision case is in order. Even though you have proven the amount of the damage to your automobile, and the necessity for the repairs, you still must establish that the culpable conduct of the other driver was the cause of the accident.

12

This you can do by your own testimony or that of a witness who saw the collision.

ADJOURNMENTS

Adjournments in Small Claims Court are discouraged. Only the judge can grant an adjournment.

If you are going to ask for an adjournment, notify the other party in advance. Either you or someone on your behalf should appear in court to explain to the judge why you cannot be ready for trial. If you do not have a good excuse, your request may be denied and, if you are not ready to go to trial, your case may be dismissed, or if you are the defendant, an award may be made against you without your having been heard.

THE SMALL CLAIMS TRIAL

Whether you are a plaintiff or defendant in a small claims case, you should arrive at the court on the day of trial no later than 9:15 A. M. since the calendar is called at 9:30 A. M. Outside of each courtroom is a bulletin board upon which the small claims calendar is placed. You should examine the calendar to determine whether your case is listed. If your case is not listed, you should inquire at the clerk's office as to the reason for it absence.

If your case is on the calendar, find a seat in the courtroom and await the arrival of the judge. When the judge takes the bench, either the judge or the clerk will call the calendar. When your name is called, you should answer "plaintiff ready" or "defendant ready" as the case may be. Those phrases signify to the judge that you are present and ready to proceed to trial.

If the plaintiff fails to appear on the day of trial, the judge will probably dismiss the plaintiff's case.

After the call of the calendar, the judge will first hear those cases where the defendant has failed to appear. Whenever a defendant failed to appear for trial, the plaintiff is still required to present his or her case to obtain a judgment against the defendant. This is known as an "inquest". If you as plaintiff find yourself in this situation you will be required to testify and offer whatever witnesses and evidence you have by which you intend to prove your case. After this has been done, the judge will inform you either that you have obtained a judgment against the defendant in a particular amount of money, or that you have failed to prove your claim. In some instances, the judge will reserve decision and you will be notified by mail of the results of the inquest.

You must recognize the fact that there will be instances when the plaintiff will fail to recover a judgment or will obtain a lesser amount of money than originally sought in the lawsuit. The reasons for this are that the judge has honestly felt that you have failed to prove your claim or that you have only partially proven your damages.

After the inquests, the judge will proceed to hear the contested trials which are those where both parties have appeared. The plaintiff presents his or her case first and usually takes the stand as the first witness. At this time the plaintiff should also introduce in evidence those documents and records intended to assist in the proof of the claim. After the plaintiff has testified the defendant then has the opportunity to cross-examine the plaintiff, that is to say, the defendant may, ask the plaintiff questions pertinent to the case.

The plaintiff may also call witnesses to give testimony and as with the plaintiff's testimony, the defendant may cross -examine those witnesses. There is no set order in which persons on one side or the other are required to testify and it may be that the plaintiff may prefer to have a witness testify first rather than oneself.

After the plaintiff has put in his case, the defendant then has the opportunity to testify and to present witnesses and to offer evidence supporting the defense and counterclaim, if any. The plaintiff then will have the same opportunity that has been afforded the defendant to cross-examine the defendant and the witnesses.

After both sides have rested, the judge will do one of two things. He will either announce the identity of the party who has won the case and the amount of the judgment or will inform the parties that the decision is reserved, which means, that the parties will be informed at a later time by mail of the results of the trial.

SETTLEMENTS

The parties to a small claims suit are encouraged to settle their cases prior to trial wherever possible. A case is settled when the defendant offers an amount of money to the plaintiff in satisfaction of the claim which offer is accepted and the money is actually paid. In many cases, the amount agreed upon is something less than the amount sought by the plaintiff in the action.

There are good reasons for settlements. You must understand that one of the parties to the suit will lose. While the small claims trial is informal, it is nevertheless a lawsuit. there is a victor and a vanquished. While you may honestly believe that you are entitled to recover from you opponent, the judge who conducts the trial may not share your confidence in your case and may rule against you. That is one reason why a reasonable offer of settlement should be seriously considered.

If you have settled your case before the day of trial and received your money, you should promptly notify the court by mail of that fact. If you have not received the money by the day of trial you should appear as if no offer of settlement has been made at all, otherwise your case might be dismissed.

If you receive an offer of settlement on the day of trial which you decided to accept but the defendant does not have the money with them to pay you or you would like additional time to consider the offer, you should inform the judge of the pending settlement and he will adjourn the case to a future day "subject to settlement". If the defendant does not pay you, or you decide not to accept the offer, then come to court on the adjourned date and be prepared to proceed to trial. If payment is made, both parties should notify the court by mail so the case can be re-corded"settled" on the adjourned date.

MAY YOU APPEAL?

If you are dissatisfied with the judgment rendered in your case and

15

believe that justice was not done, you may appeal from the judgment. Rendered by a judge (an arbitrators award is not appealable).You may not appeal if you failed to appear for trial or upon any ground other than your assertion that substantial justice was not done in your case. The fact that you believe that there were technical defects of one kind or another in the trial will be of no assistance to you. The appellate court will consider the judgment reached only in the light of whether the trial judge rendered a just and fair decision.

Before taking an appeal, there are some things you should know. The prosecution of an appeal requires a certain amount of legal skill which is probably a bit more than most layman can muster. If you lack that skill, you may need an attorney who will undoubtedly charge you a fee.

Another important requirement in taking an appeal is that you must purchase the minutes of the trial. This is a typewritten record of what has transpired at your trial. If the minutes were taken by a court reporter, contact the chief court reporter's office at (516) 572-2180, to obtain an estimate of the cost of the minutes. If a tape recorder was utilized for the case, correspond your request to the clerk of the Court for information regarding a transcription of the tape recorded hearing.

You should also bear in mind that the mere fact that you commence an appeal by the service and filing of a notice of appeal and paying the required fee does not stay your opponent from attempting to collect the judgment. To obtain a stay in connection with an appeal, the party who is appealing must file with the clerk of the Court an undertaking given by a surety in the amount of the judgment providing that if the judgment appealed from or any part of it is affirmed, or the appeal is dismissed, the appellant shall pay the amount directed to be paid by the judgment, or in lieu of filing an undertaking you may stay the collection of the judgment by depositing cash with the clerk in the amount of the judgment. The small claims "Notice of Appeal" forms are available at the clerk's office.

If you desire to represent yourself in the appeal, a notice of appeal must be served by someone, other than a party to the action, over the age of eighteen, by regular first class mail, upon your adversary within the thirty (30) day period and the original of said notice of appeal filed with the Court together with proof of service. There is a $25 fee for filing the notice of appel.

16

Some people do prosecute their own appeals without counsel. It requires determination and skill. If you decide to appeal, you must do so within 30 days after judgment. Visit the clerk's office as soon after you receive notice of the results of your case. The clerk will advise you as to the initial step in taking the appeal but beyond that advice, the clerks are not equipped nor permitted to give legal advice.

THE JUDGMENT –HOW TO COLLECT IT

After the trial or inquest, the court will notify the parties of the judge's decision. This is known as the judgment. It will inform the parties either

1.   That the plaintiff is awarded judgment against one or more defendants in a specific amount of money, or,
2.   that the defendant is awarded judgment dismissing the plaintiff's claim, and/or
3.   that the defendant is awarded judgment against the plaintiff on defendant's counterclaim in a specific sum of money.

If, after obtaining a judgment you do not receive your money, within a reasonable amount of time (2 - 3 weeks) from the judgment debtor, it is advisable to contact the debtor. If the debtor informs you that he or she does not intend to pay, or you receive the impression that the debtor is avoiding the obligation to pay, or you are unable to reach the debtor after several attempts to do so, you should take steps to obtain an Execution. An Execution is a legal document which authorizes the sheriff to collect the judgment amount for you.

You can assist the Sheriff in collecting your judgment by providing information identifying property of the judgment debtor. The identity of the defendant's bank accounts is a most valuable bit of information to furnish the Sheriff. Is the defendant employed? Does he or she own a car? Source of income-what are they? Answers to these questions are important if the Sheriff is to succeed in the pursuit of the judgment debtor's assets. If you obtain information of this nature, put it in writing and furnish it to the Sheriff at the time the execution is requested.

There is a law that will give you further assistance in identifying the debtor's assets. The law provides that if after you are awarded a judgment, it remains unsatisfied, the court clerk will assist you in the preparation of an information subpoena. An information subpoena is a legal document commanding the judgment debtor or some other person to answer questions about the debtor's assets and income.

17

The person served with the information subpoena is required to answer these questions in writing.

The court clerk has information subpoena forms and instructions for this purpose and will assist you in the preparation of these forms and furnish you with written instructions concerning their service and what to do with the information once it is obtained. There is a $2.00 fee for an information subpoena.

Examples of questions commonly asked in an information subpoena to be served upon a judgment debtor are

What is the name and address of your employer?

What are your weekly earnings?

What is the name and address of your bank

What is your savings account number and the balance of that account?

Examples of questions commonly asked in an information subpoena to a bank are:

Does the judgment debtor maintain an account in your bank?

What is the account number and balance of that account?

To obtain an execution you should first request the court to issue a transcript of judgment. A $5.00 fee is charged for issuing a transcript. After obtaining the transcript you should file it with the Nassau County Clerk and request that an execution be issued to the Sheriff of Nassau County. Both the Nassau County Clerk's and the Sheriff's office are located in the office building at 240 Old Country Road, Mineola, New York 11501.

You have the right to notify the appropriate state or local licensing or certifying authority of an unsatisfied judgment if it arises out of the carrying on, conducting or transaction of a licensed or certified business or if such business appears to be engaged in fraudulent or illegal acts or otherwise demonstrates fraud or illegality in carrying on, conducting or transaction of its business.

18

In addition, if the judgment debtor has two (2) prior unpaid judgments of a small claim court, which arose from the judgment debtor's trade, business, or from a repeated course of dealing or conducting business, you (judgment creditor) may have the basis for an action for treble the amount of your judgment.

NIGHT SMALL CLAIMS

You may, if you wish have the case scheduled at night; but the case must be initiated during the business hours, of 9:00 - 4:30 Monday through Friday. Night small claims trials are heard only in the District Court building at 99 Main Street, Hempstead, New York, on Tuesday, Wednesday and Thursday evenings. The judge calls the calendar at 6 P. M. and it is important for you to arrive on time.

ARBITRATION

Arbitration of small claims cases is always available in the night small claims part and at times arbitrators are available to hear cases in the 3 daytime small claims parts.

If all of the participants to a small claims case consent they may have their case heard by an arbitrator rather than by a District Court Judge. The arbitrator is an experienced attorney who serves without pay and is appointed by the Supervising Judge of the District Court to act as an arbitrator. As with small claims trials held before a District Court Judge, a party may be represented by an attorney if his case is heard by an arbitrator.

If the parties agree to arbitration, each side will have the opportunity to give testimony, introduce evidence and have witnesses give testimony to prove their case or defense, as the parties and their witnesses will be under oath or affirmation, however, the arbitrator will not be bound by the rules regarding the admissibility of evidence. Under these circumstances, experience has shown that it is somewhat easier for a party to present their case or to defend themselves without being concerned about technical rules of evidence.

If the case is heard by an arbitrator, the parties will be bound by the decision and no appeal can be had from it. The arbitrator's decision, or award as it is known, is as binding upon all concerned as if it were a judgment of the court and as a matter of fact, when the arbitrator files the written decision with the court, it becomes a judgment of the District Court. It may then be enforced in the same manner as any judgment obtained after trial before a judge.

MEDIATION

At each small claims court location certified mediators are available to assist litigants in settling their case. The mediation sessions are non-judgmental and non-adversarial. Your appearance before a mediator is voluntary. If a settlement is agreed to, the mediator will prepare a written agreement detailing the terms and conditions of the settlement and will file it with the court. This agreement becomes a legally binding document. If after conferencing your case with a mediator, a settlement cannot be reached, you may return to the courtroom for trial.

YOUR CONDUCT THROUGHOUT THE CASE

Keep cool. It frequently happens that the circumstances giving rise to your claim or the fact that you are being sued has made you upset and angry. If you give in to your feelings, it will not help your case. This is particularly true during the course of the trial. Do your best to be composed and present your case in a calm and business-like fashion.

Unfortunately there are things about a lawsuit that sometimes cause annoyance. On the day of trial you may discover that your case is listed towards the end of the calendar and the judge is unable to reach you until the afternoon. This cannot be avoided since a certain number of cases must be listed for each day it is pure chance that has placed you towards the end of the day's business. Use the waiting time to advantage by sitting in the courtroom and observing the other trials. You may learn something that you can put to good use in your own case.

By and large the people associated with the District Court are fair minded, patient people. While we would hope it were not so, on rare occasions, one of them may become ill mannered. Being human they are not at their best every day. Should this occur during the course of your case, please accept our sincere apologies. Your best response to such conduct, of course is your own good nature. It may very well save the day.

DEFINITIONS

adjournment	Postponement of case to another date
adult	person eighteen years of age or older
calendar	list of cases to be heard by the judge on a particular day
cause of action	claim by one person against another
counterclaim	claim by defendant against plaintiff seeking damages
cross-examination	asking questions of opposing party and their witnesses
damages	the amount of money a party seeks to recover in a lawsuit
defendant	person or business who is sued
execution	legal document authorizing Sheriff to seize personal property of a judgment debtor
infant	person under eighteen years of age
inquest	hearing before a judge of party's proof of claim where his opponent has failed to appear
judgment	legal document setting forth the outcome of a lawsuit
judgment debtor	person against whom a judgment has been obtained who has not fully paid the amount they are liable for

22

lawsuit	process by which one person sues another in a court - the words "action" and "suit" have the same meaning as lawsuit
party	either plaintiff or defendant
plaintiff	person who sues another
Prima Facie Evidence	Evidence that is adequate to prove a particular fact
subpoena	legal document commanding a witness to come to court to testify
summons	legal document when served upon a defendant begins a lawsuit
testimony	statements made under oath in a court by a party or a witness
witness	person who testifies in court on behalf of plaintiff or defendant

DISTRICT COURT PERSONNEL

Eileen Bianchi
Chief Clerk

Deputy Chief Clerk   Robert M. Henken
Deputy Chief Clerk   Kenneth Roll

1st District Civil Clerk- Hempstead   William K. Breien, Jr.
99 Main Street
Hempstead, New York 11550
(516) 572-2262

Hicksville Part Clerk   Dona Pratesi
87 Bethpage Road
Hicksville, New York 11801
(516) 571-7090

Great Neck Part Clerk   Walter Novinsky
435 Middle Neck Road
Great Neck, New York 11023
(516) 571-8400

Revised 3/99

Appendix 3

A GUIDE TO SMALL CLAIMS COURT

- ## New York City

- ## Nassau County

- ## Suffolk County

2001-2002

Judith S. Kaye
Chief Judge

Jonathan Lippman
Chief Administrative Judge

INTRODUCTION

In 1984, as part of the Small Claims Judges' Committee for the New York City Civil Court, Judge Beverly Cohen and I wrote a new "Guide to the Small Claims Court."

At that time, the book was a guide for New York City only. This year I am pleased to inform you that I have included Nassau and Suffolk Counties. This guide, also known as the "Blue Book," contains information you will need to commence an action in any Small Claims Court within New York City, Nassau and Suffolk Counties. However, wherever there is a difference in procedure between the courts, the proper procedure for each court will be noted in bold type.

Small Claims Court is known as the "People's Court," primarily because it is user friendly. It is a court where litigants, if they choose, can try their cases without the necessity of an attorney. Therefore, this guide was written to assist the self-represented litigant. In addition to reflecting recent changes in the statutes and rules, I have divided this guide into four sections: how to start your action; how to proceed with the collection of a judgment; important governmental agencies; and locations of all the Small Claims Courts in New York City, Nassau and Suffolk Counties.

Immediately following this page is a "quick overview" page which will allow you to determine who can use the Small Claims Court.
Finally, I hope this guide will help facilitate your Small Claims Court experience.

Joseph A. J. Gebbia
Chief Clerk Small Claims Court
Civil Court of the City of New York

QUICK OVERVIEW

Read the appropriate section in this book for detailed information

- You must be 18 or over to sue
- Sue for money only - up to $3000
- Only an individual claimant can sue *
- Simple form available at clerk's office. State your name, address, reason for suit, amount, who you want to sue (defendant), and defendant's address.
- Fee is $10 for claims up to $1000 - - $15 for claims up to $3000
- Clerk will give you a court date and notify the defendant. Court starts at either 9:30 a.m. or 6:30 P.M. (6:00 p.m. in **Suffolk County**)
- **New York City** Small Claims is primarily an evening court (6:30 P.M.)
  Day court is available at 9:30 a.m.(ask the Clerk for details)
- **Nassau and Suffolk** are primarily day time courts - 9:30 a.m.
- If the defendant can't be served by mail, the clerk will give you additional instructions

---

* A partnership may bring a lawsuit in Small Claims Court in District Court or City Court in Nassau County and in Suffolk County District Court.

The **New York City** book is available in Spanish and Chinese versions. There is also a commercial guide for corporations, and partnerships.

TABLE OF CONTENTS

PART I - ABOUT SMALL CLAIMS COURT

PART II - COLLECTIONS

PART III - IMPORTANT GOVERNMENT OFFICES

PART IV - LOCATIONS

PART I - ABOUT SMALL CLAIMS COURT

WHAT IS SMALL CLAIMS COURT?

The Small Claims Court is a simple, inexpensive and informal court where individuals can sue for money only, up to $3,000, without a lawyer. Claims for more than $3,000 may not be brought in a Small Claims Court; they must be brought in another part of the court or in a different court. If you have a claim for damages for more than $3000, you cannot "split" it into two or more claims to meet the $3000 limit. (i.e. bring one $3000 claim and another $1500 claim to recover damages at $4500.)

Since the Small Claims Court hears suits for money only, you cannot sue in Small Claims Court to force a person or business to fix a damaged item. You also cannot sue in Small Claims Court to make a person or business fulfill a promise made in an advertisement, and you cannot sue for pain and suffering.

If you want to sue an agency of the **City of New York**, the Small Claims Clerk can provide you with a list of addresses for all the New York City agencies. First you must notify the agency within 90 days of the occurrence. When you deliver your notice to the agency you will receive a claim number. You must wait 30 days for the City to make an offer of settlement or to deny your claim. If the City denies your claim, you then can proceed to the Small Claims Court office to begin your small claims case. You have one year and 90 days from the occurrence to commence your small claims action.
If you do not notify the City within 90 days of the occurrence, your case may be dismissed.

You can also sue a **municipality (town, village, city) or county** in Small Claims Court. However, the law requires you first to notify the municipality of your intention to sue. That notice must be given to the municipality within 90 days after the occurrence of the incident that is the subject of your suit. You must wait 30 days for the municipality to make an offer of settlement or to deny your claim. If the municipality denies your claim you can then proceed to the Small Claims Court office to begin your small claims case. You have one year and ninety days from the occurrence to commence your small claims action. *If you do not notify the municipality within 90 days of the incident, your case may be dismissed.*

You must go to the Court of Claims Court to commence a lawsuit against the State of New York or an agency of the State of New York.

WHO CAN USE SMALL CLAIMS COURT?

Anyone 18 years of age or over can sue in Small Claims Court. If you are younger than 18, your parent or guardian may sue on your behalf. Only an individual can sue in Small Claims Court. Corporations, partnerships, associations, or assignees cannot sue in Small Claims Court.[1] They can, however, be sued in Small Claims Court. If you are a corporation, partnership or assignee, you can sue in the Commercial Small Claims Part. Ask the clerk for the Commercial Small Claims booklet.

If you sue in Small Claims Court, you are called the claimant; if you are sued, you are the defendant. You can sue more than one defendant at the same time if necessary.

---

[1] A partnership may bring a lawsuit in Small Claims Court in the District Court or City Court of Nassau and in the Suffolk County District Court.

If you are sued and you believe that someone else (a third-party) is responsible for the amount claimed, you may be able to bring that party into the lawsuit as an additional defendant. Contact the clerk of the Small Claims Court for information about a "third-party action."

A corporation may authorize an attorney, officer, director, or employee of the corporation to appear on their behalf to defend a small claims action.

DO I NEED AN ATTORNEY?

Because the Small Claims Court procedures are informal, you do not need an attorney to represent you. You may, however, choose to hire an attorney to represent you whether you are a claimant or defendant.

WHERE ARE SMALL CLAIMS COURTS LOCATED?

In **New York City**, Small Claims Court is part of the Civil Court of the City of New York. There is at least one Small Claims Court in each of the five boroughs of New York City. See Part IV of this booklet for locations and hours.

In **Nassau County**, the City and District Courts have Small Claims Courts. See Part IV for location and hours.

In **Suffolk County**, the District Courts have Small Claims Courts. See Part IV of this booklet for location and hours.

WHICH SMALL CLAIMS COURT SHOULD I USE?.

In **New York City**, you may file your small claim in the Small Claims Court of the New York City Civil Court located in the county where <u>you live</u> or in the Small Claims Court in the county where the <u>defendant resides or works or has a place of business.</u>

In the **<u>City Court or District Court</u>** of **<u>Nassau County</u> or the <u>District Court</u>** of **<u>Suffolk County,</u>** you may file your small claim in the Small Claims Court located in the court district <u>where the defendant resides or works or has a place of business.</u>

CAN I HAVE AN INTERPRETER?

If you or any of your witnesses will need an interpreter during your court hearing, tell the Small Claims Clerk when you file your small claim. The clerk will arrange to have an "official" interpreter available for you or your witnesses at the time of your hearing.

WHEN IS SMALL CLAIMS COURT IN SESSION?

In **New York City,** Small Claims Court sessions generally are held during the evening, beginning at 6:30 p.m. You should arrive 30 or more minutes early because you will have to go through magnetometers for security reasons, and this may delay your arrival. If you are a senior citizen (65 years of age or older) or you are disabled, or if you work during the evening, the Small Claims Clerk will schedule your case during a daytime session.

Courts **outside New York City** may hold Small Claims Court sessions during the day or the evening, or both. You should ask the Small Claims Court Clerk in the court where you will file your small claim for the days and times when Small Claims Court is in session.

4

HOW DO I START MY SMALL CLAIMS CASE?

You, or someone on your behalf, must go to the Small Claims Court to file your claim. You may file by mail if you live outside the City of New York and want to sue a party within the City of New York. Contact the Small Claims Clerk in the county where the defendant lives, works or has a place of business. The Small Claims Clerk will provide you with the necessary form. This form will require you to give a brief statement about your claim and a description of the incident that is the basis of your small claim. Also the name(s) and address(es) of the party(ies) who you are suing. You must give the Small Claims Court Clerk the defendant's street address. A post office box only, is not acceptable. You will be required to pay a $10 filing fee if your claim is $1,000 or less. If your claim is more than $1,000 you must pay a $15 filing fee.

You must be the proper person to sue in Small Claims Court. For example, if you are involved in an accident while driving an automobile that is not registered in your name, you cannot sue for the damage caused to the automobile during the accident. Only the registered owner of the automobile can sue for the damage caused to the automobile.

Do I Have to Know the Defendant's Correct or "Legal" Name?

When you file your small claim, you must give theCourt Clerk the name and address of the person or business you want to sue. You can obtain the correct or "legal" name of a business by contacting the office of the County Clerk in the county where the business is located. You do not need to know the correct or legal name of a business or a person who operates a business to file your claim. You can provide any name used by the business or by the person who operates

5

the business. If you learn the defendant's correct or legal name later, you can give it to the Small Claims Court Clerk before your trial or during your trial. However, if you get a judgment against a business it will be easier to collect if you know the correct legal name.

WHO TELLS THE DEFENDANT ABOUT MY CLAIM?

After your claim is filed, the Small Claims Court Clerk will "serve" a notice of your claim by sending it to the defendant. The notice of claim tells the defendant when to appear in Small Claims Court, and includes a brief statement of your claim and the amount of money you are requesting.

The notice of your claim will be sent to the defendant by certified mail and by ordinary first class mail. If the notice sent by ordinary first class mail is not returned by the post office within 21 days as undeliverable, the defendant is presumed to have received notice of your claim, even if the notice of claim sent by certified mail has not been delivered.

If the post office cannot deliver the notice of your claim (for example, the defendant may have moved without leaving a forwarding address), the court clerk will give you a new hearing date and will tell you how to arrange for personal delivery of the notice to the defendant. Anyone who is not a party to the small claim and who is 18 years of age or older (including a friend or relative) can personally deliver the notice of claim to the defendant.   The claimant or any other party to the action, may not serve the notice of claim personally on the defendant.

If the notice of your claim cannot be served on the defendant within 4 months after you filed your claim, your

6

claim will be dismissed. If you learn new information about the defendant's location at a later date, you can file your claim again.

A small claims case will not proceed to trial until the defendant has been served with a notice of your claim.

WHAT IS A COUNTERCLAIM?

A "counterclaim" is a claim filed against you by the person you have named in your small claim. The counterclaim must be for money only. The amount of the counterclaim cannot be more than $3,000. Any counterclaim for more than $3,000 must be brought in another part of the court or in a different court.

The defendant may file a counterclaim within five days after receiving the notice of your claim and must pay a $3 filing fee plus the cost of mailing the counterclaim to you. The defendant may also file a counterclaim on the day of the hearing. If the defendant files a counterclaim on the day of the hearing and you are not prepared to defend against the counterclaim, you can ask the Judge to postpone the hearing until another day. In some cases, the Judge might decide to delay the hearing, even if you do not ask for an adjournment.

If you receive notice of a counterclaim before the date of your hearing, you must be prepared to present your claim and defend against the counterclaim on the day of the hearing.

CAN I CHANGE THE DATE OF MY HEARING?

Adjournments in the Small Claims Court are discouraged. Only the Judge decides if an adjournment is to be granted.

How Do I Ask For an Adjournment?

Adjournments by telephone are not available in **New York City** or in **Nassau** and **Suffolk Counties.**

If you are going to ask for an adjournment, you should notify the court by mail before the scheduled date of your trial (if possible), and mail a copy of your letter to the other party as well. On the day of the trial, either you or someone else should appear in the Small Claims Court to explain to the Judge why you are not prepared for trial.

If you do not have a good excuse, your request for an adjournment may be denied. If your request for an adjournment is denied and you are not ready to start your hearing, your small claim may be dismissed. If you are the defendant and you do not appear, the Judge may award the claimant an inquest (default judgment) against you, even though the Judge has not heard your side of the story.

HOW DO I PREPARE FOR MY HEARING?

Before the date of the hearing, you should gather all the evidence that supports your claim or your defense. Evidence may include: photographs, a written agreement, an itemized bill or invoice marked "paid," receipts, written estimates of the cost of services or repairs (you must present two itemized estimates for services or repairs), a canceled check, a damaged item or article of clothing, or letters or other written documents.

Who Can Testify at My Hearing?

Testimony is a sworn statement made by you or another person, given in court, before the Judge or Arbitrator. Anyone who knows something about your claim, including you, can testify during the hearing. For example, a person who saw what happened, or someone who has special or expert knowledge and experience concerning the subject of your claim, can be a witness at the hearing.

How Can I Get an Expert Witness to Testify?

The testimony of a person who has special or expert knowledge and experience concerning the subject of your claim may be necessary for you to prove your case. For example, if your claim involves the quality of medical care, you must find a doctor who is willing to give an opinion, in court, about the quality of the care you received. While you might find an expert witness who will testify at no cost to you, it is more likely that you will have to pay for an expert witness' testimony. You cannot use a subpoena to compel an expert witness to appear.

What Can I Do if a Witness Will Not Testify Voluntarily?

If a witness will not testify voluntarily, you can ask the Small Claims Court Clerk to issue a "subpoena." A subpoena is a legal document that commands the named person to appear in court to testify or to produce records. The Small Claims Court Clerk will assist you in preparing the necessary documents.

You must arrange for service of the subpoena on the appropriate person. The person subpoenaed is entitled to a

9

$15 witness fee and in some cases travel expenses, which must be paid at the time the subpoena is served. You are responsible for paying these fees. Anyone who is not a party to the small claim and who is 18 years of age or older (including a friend or relative) can serve the subpoena. As the claimant or the defendant, you cannot serve the subpoena.

A subpoena can be served any time before the hearing. However, a witness should be given a "reasonable" amount of time before s/he must appear. Generally, it is considered reasonable to serve the subpoena at least five (5) days before the hearing date. This will allow the person subpoenaed sufficient time to prepare the items you request or appear at the hearing.

WHAT SHOULD I DO ON THE DAY OF MY HEARING?

On the day of the hearing, you should arrive at the courthouse at least 30 minutes before the Small Claims Court session begins. When you arrive at the courthouse, look for a Small Claims Court calendar. Usually it is posted outside the Small Claims courtroom. Your case will be listed by your last name and by the last name of the defendant. If your case is not listed on the Small Claims Court calendar, or if a calendar is not posted outside the Small Claims courtroom, speak to the court clerk.

If a claimant does not arrive at the courthouse on time, the claimant's case may be dismissed. If the defendant does not arrive at the courthouse on time, the Judge may hear and decide the case based only on evidence provided by the claimant.

What Do I Do When the Clerk is Calling the Calendar ?

The Small Claims Court Clerk will announce your case and call your name. When your name is called, you should stand, repeat your name, and answer "ready," or if you are not ready to begin and instead need to ask for an adjournment, or if you have some other request, you should tell the judge at this time by saying "application." If you and the party you are suing are both ready, the case will go forward to trial.

Should I Choose a Judge or an Arbitrator?

In **New York City** and **Nassau County**, you can choose a Judge or Arbitrator to try your claim. In **Suffolk County**, your case will be sent directly to an Arbitrator for trial.

An Arbitrator is an experienced attorney who is specially trained to hear and decide small claims. Because there are more Arbitrators available to hear cases than there are Judges, an Arbitrator will hear your claim more quickly. The hearing before an Arbitrator is informal. The Arbitrator applies the same law to your case as a Judge would apply.

One important difference between a Judge and an Arbitrator is that an Arbitrator's decision cannot be appealed because there is no official record of the proceedings. A trial before a Judge will result in a decision that can be appealed, as the trial will be heard with a court reporter or recording device, therefore there will be a court record necessary to process an appeal.

Can I Have a Jury Decide My Claim?

As the claimant in a small claims action, you have waived your right to a jury trial. A defendant, however, may demand a trial by jury. If you are the defendant and you demand a jury trial you will have to pay a jury fee of $55 and also must pay $50 to the court for any costs that the court awards to the claimant. A defendant who requests a jury trial also must submit an "affidavit," a sworn notarized statement, in which the defendant must state that the claim involves one or more factual questions that must be decided by a jury and that the request for a jury trial is made in good faith. See the court clerk if you request a jury trial.

WHAT HAPPENS DURING MY TRIAL?

The claimant has the burden of proving the claim and any damages. The claimant's case is presented first. After being sworn as a witness, the claimant will tell his or her version of the incident. All papers or other evidence should be shown at this time. When the claimant has finished testifying, the Judge or Arbitrator or the defendant may ask some questions to clarify matters. Other witnesses can be presented in support of the claim, and they, also, can be questioned. All witnesses will be sworn in.

The Defendant Tells His or Her story

After the claimant has offered all the evidence that supports the claim, the defendant will take an oath and tell his/her side of the story. The defendant may offer papers and other evidence, and can call other witnesses to testify on his/her behalf. The defendant and any witnesses who testify for the defendant also must take an oath to tell the truth and can be questioned by the Judge or Arbitrator and by the claimant.

If You Are Suing a Business

During the hearing, the Judge or Arbitrator should determine a defendant's true business name. If the legal name of the business is different from the name that is written on your notice of claim, ask the court to have the name on the notice of claim corrected by the clerk.

Disclosure of Assets

If you are the claimant, it is your responsibility to collect information on the defendant's assets - property that the defendant owns - in the event you receive a judgment in your favor and the defendant does not pay [SEE PART II - COLLECTION in this booklet]. You can ask the Judge or Arbitrator to question the defendant about his/her assets. The defendant's assets are property, such as a car, a house or money, that can be used to pay your judgment. The Judge or Arbitrator can direct the defendant not to sell or give away those assets before paying any amount you are awarded.

The Decision

After the claimant and the defendant have offered all their evidence, the Judge or Arbitrator will normally "reserve decision," which means that the Judge or Arbitrator needs time to evaluate the evidence and that the decision will be mailed to the claimant and the defendant after the hearing. In rare cases, the Judge or Arbitrator may announce the decision immediately after the hearing.

WHAT HAPPENS IF ONE PARTY DOES NOT APPEAR?

If the Claimant Does Not Appear

If the claimant does not appear in court on the court date, when the small claims case is called, the claim will be dismissed.

If the Defendant Does Not Appear

If the defendant does not appear, the court will direct an "inquest." This means the Judge or Arbitrator will hear your case even though the defendant is not present. If the claimant presents enough evidence to establish his/her case, the Judge or Arbitrator will award a "default judgment" against the defendant.

If a Default Judgment is Awarded

If a default judgment is awarded because the defendant did not appear, the defendant may ask the court to re-open the case so that s/he can offer evidence in defense of the small claim. A defendant who does not appear on the scheduled date and then asks the court to re-open the small claim must have a valid excuse for not appearing, "excusable default", and must be able to show that s/he has a valid defense. A Small Claims Court Clerk will assist in preparing the necessary papers to ask the Judge to re-open the case. The Small Claims Court Clerk also will set a date when the claimant and the defendant must return to court.

When the claimant and the defendant return to court, the Judge will decide whether to re-open the case. If the Judge does re-open the case, the claimant and the defendant

14

must be ready to present their evidence at that time. However, the Judge may decide to adjourn the trial to a later date.

CAN I SETTLE MY SMALL CLAIM BEFORE THE JUDGE HEARS THE EVIDENCE?

Although you may be confident that you will win your small claim, the Judge or Arbitrator may make a decision that you do not like. It is almost always better for the claimant and the defendant to settle their dispute themselves. The claimant and the defendant can agree to settle the small claim before the court date and before the Judge or Arbitrator hears the evidence, and even during the hearing.

If the Case is Settled Before the Court Date

If the claimant and the defendant settle the small claim before the court date, and any money requested has been paid, the claimant should notify the Small Claims Court Clerk by mail. The claimant and the defendant then do not have to appear in court.

Adjournment Pending Settlement

If the claimant and the defendant settle the small claim before the hearing date, but the money has not been paid, or if the claimant and the defendant expect to settle the dispute, but still are negotiating the terms of the settlement, the claimant must appear in court on the scheduled hearing date so that the small claim is not dismissed. The claimant should ask the Judge for "an adjournment pending settlement," and a new hearing date will be scheduled. If the claimant and the defendant then cannot settle the small claim, they must appear in court on the new scheduled hearing date prepared to present their evidence to the Judge or an Arbitrator.

In the **New York City** Small Claims Court, if both parties appear on the trial date, and request the case be heard by the Judge, but the court realizes that the case cannot be heard on that date, the parties may be asked to participate in a pre-trial conference. The purpose of this conference is to attempt to settle the small claims case. If the case is not settled, it will be adjourned to the next available court date.

CAN I APPEAL THE JUDGE'S DECISION?

When you "appeal" a decision, you ask a higher court to review it for any error. You can appeal a Judge's decision. You cannot appeal an Arbitrator's decision.

Few small claims decisions are appealed, and very few appeals are successful. The appellate court will consider only whether substantial justice was done between the parties. The appellate court will not reverse a small claims decision because a technical mistake was made during the hearing.

You may need the help of an attorney to appeal your small claims decision. Because the amounts involved in small claims are small, the expense of appealing your small claims decision may be greater than the amount awarded. In addition, the appealing party must purchase a typed transcript of the hearing for the appellate court.

If you decide to appeal, you must file a Notice of Appeal and pay the required fee within 30 days after the judgment is entered. Consult the Small Claims Court Clerk for further information.

The party who appeals a small claims decision must pay any amount awarded unless a bond or undertaking is paid to the Small Claims Court to guarantee payment of the judgment if the appeal is lost. If you receive notice of an appeal, you should call the Small Claims Court to find out if a bond or an undertaking has been paid. If a bond or an undertaking has not been paid, you can begin to collect your judgment immediately.

DO I HAVE TO GO TO SMALL CLAIMS COURT TO SOLVE MY PROBLEM?

No. There are Community Dispute Resolution Centers available in every county of New York State. These centers serve as a community resource where you and another person can discuss and solve your dispute through mediation. Mediation is a confidential, informal procedure guided by a neutral third party called a mediator. A mediator is trained to help people resolve their disputes. A mediator does not offer an opinion about the problem or about whether one side or the other might succeed in court. A mediator cannot make a decision. A mediator helps you and another person to identify the problem, explore different ways to solve your problem and to find a solution that is acceptable to both people involved. A mediation often results in a written agreement between the people involved.

There normally is no charge or filing fee. Your case will be scheduled quickly at a time and place convenient to the people involved. You can find the address and telephone number for the community dispute resolution center near you in your telephone book. You can also get a brochure at the Small Claims Court office that lists local dispute resolution centers.

In **New York City,** during the school year, law school students from various law schools are available in the Small

Claims Court to mediate small claims. These law students are trained by the court to assist litigants to mediate their disputes. If one of the parties asks for the Court and the Court determines that the case will not be heard by the Judge you will be asked to mediate your case. If your case is not settled, you will be given a date to return for trial. Arbitrators are also available, after they have completed their trials, to mediate your small claim.

PART II - COLLECTING YOUR JUDGMENT

WHAT DO I DO IF I WIN?

If the claimant wins, the court will enter a judgment for a sum of money. The claimant then must "enforce" or collect the amount of the judgment. The court also may require the claimant to take certain action - for example, to return damaged merchandise to the defendant - before entering judgment.

How Can I Collect My Judgment?

Both sides will receive a "Notice of Judgment" from the court. The Notice of Judgment will include the Judge's or Arbitrator's decision, as well as, information about the location of the sheriff's office and ways to collect your judgment. You must read all the information, printed on both sides of the Notice of Judgment, before you can begin your collection efforts. In **Suffolk County**, you will receive an Arbitrator's award, and the collection information is printed on one side only. Winning a judgment does not guarantee you will collect your money. A money judgment is legally enforceable for 20 years.

The person awarded a judgment is called the judgment creditor, and the person who owes the amount awarded is called the judgment debtor.

Contact the judgment debtor and request payment of the judgment amount. If the judgment debtor refuses to pay the judgment amount, you may need the services of an enforcement officer.

19

What is an Enforcement Officer?

An enforcement officer can seize a judgment debtor's assets to pay your judgment. The Sheriff is employed by the county, and is an enforcement officer. A City Marshal is also an enforcement officer. A City Marshal is not employed by the government, but instead works independently. In **New York City** the clerk can provide you with a list of City Marshals or you can consult the telephone book.

How Does an Enforcement Officer Work?

In **New York City** when you contact an enforcement officer, ask the officer to request an "execution" from the court. The execution allows the officer to seize a judgment debtor's property or money. Before the officer asks the court for an execution, s/he must know what assets the judgment debtor has and where they can be found. It is your responsibility to provide this information, the enforcement officer will not look for the judgment debtor's assets without your assistance.

In **Nassau and Suffolk Counties** instructions on how to enforce your judgment will be included with the decision of the court.

Will I Have to Pay the Enforcement Officer?

You will have to pay certain fees for the enforcement officer's services. For example, you must pay the enforcement officer a mileage fee in advance for a property execution. You may have to pay up to $50 in advance for an income execution. An income execution orders the judgment debtor's employer to pay a certain amount of the debtor's wages to you until the full amount of the judgment is paid.

Sometimes these fees can be added to the amount of the judgment to be paid by the judgment debtor. If you reach a settlement with the judgment debtor after you hire an enforcement officer, you will not recover the fees already paid, additionally, you will be responsible to the enforcement officer for 5% of the settlement amount. This is true even if you negotiate the settlement without any assistance from the enforcement officer.

HOW DO I FIND A JUDGMENT DEBTOR'S ASSETS?

You can use an "information subpoena" to find a judgment debtor's assets. An information subpoena is a legal document that tells a person, corporation or other business to answer certain questions about where the judgment debtor's assets can be found. There are two parts to an information subpoena: The court's direction to provide information and the questions about the judgment debtor's assets. You can use pre-printed questions or you can write your own questions. An information subpoena may be sent to the judgment debtor and to any person, corporation or other business that you believe has knowledge about the judgment debtor's assets - for example, the telephone or other utility company, an employer, a landlord or a bank.

The clerk will provide an information subpoena for a $2 fee. You can also purchase the necessary forms from a legal stationary store or copy the necessary forms from a legal forms book that can be found in any law library.

The information subpoena must be signed by the Court Clerk. After the form is signed, send the information subpoena, two copies of the written questions and a self-addressed envelope with the correct amount of postage attached.

You can send these documents to the judgment debtor by regular mail or by certified mail, return receipt requested.

Are There Any Other Ways to Find a Judgment Debtor's Assets?

A simple way to improve the chances of collecting your judgment is to learn the name and address of the bank where the defendant keeps a savings or checking account. One way to do this is to look at the back of a canceled check you or a friend may have given to the defendant. With this information, the enforcement officer can seize money in the defendant's account and use the funds to satisfy your judgment.

You can check with the New York State Department of Motor Vehicles to find out if the judgment debtor owns a car. If the judgment debtor owns the car, the enforcement officer can take the car and sell it to pay your judgment. You must give the enforcement officer the model, year, license plate number and location of the car. If the judgment debtor borrowed money to buy the car, that loan must be paid before you can get any money. Also, you will have to pay towing and storage fees in advance to the enforcement officer. These fees can typically be $150 or more.

What if the Judgment Debtor Owns Real Estate?

If the judgment debtor owns real estate, it can be sold to pay your judgment. The Court Clerk can tell you how to determine if the judgment debtor owns a particular piece of real estate. If s/he does own real estate, you must get a "transcript of judgment" from the clerk and file it with the County Clerk. Then you must contact the Sheriff about selling the real estate to pay your judgment. It will be your responsibility to prepare the papers to sell the property. The Sheriff will deduct fees and expenses from the proceeds of the sale, and also will have to pay any mortgage, tax liens or prior judgments owed by the judgment debtor before your judgment can be paid.

The Sheriff is the only enforcement officer who can take or sell real estate.

Are There Other Ways to Make a Judgment Debtor Pay?

Claims Based on Motor Vehicle Ownership

If your small claim was based on the judgment debtor's ownership or operation of a car, the New York State Department of Motor Vehicles may suspend the judgment debtor's driver's license and registration privileges until your judgment is paid. The amount of your judgment must be more than $1,000, and it must be unpaid for more than 15 days. The Small Claims Court Clerk can give you more information about this enforcement method.

Licensing Agencies

If your small claim relates to the judgment debtor's business, and the business is licensed or certified by a state or local authority, you can notify that authority if your judgment is not paid within 35 days after the judgment debtor received notice of the judgment. Failure to pay a judgment may be considered by the licensing authority as grounds for revoking, suspending, or refusing to grant or renew a license to operate a business. You will find a list of prominent licensing or certifying authorities for New York City, Nassau and Suffolk Counties, in PART IV of this guide.

The Judgment Debtor Has Failed to Pay Three or More Judgments

If a judgment debtor fails to pay three or more recorded judgments despite having sufficient resources to pay them, you may be able to sue the defendant for triple damages. Check with the Small Claims Court Clerk to find out if the judgment debtor is listed in the index of unsatisfied judgments maintained by the Small Claims Court.

Fraudulent or Illegal Conduct

If the judgment debtor is a business that the court finds to be engaged in fraudulent or illegal conduct, you have the right to notify the Attorney General and, if the business is licensed, the appropriate licensing authority as well.

PART III - IMPORTANT GOVERNMENT OFFICES

The Department of Consumer Affairs enforces the Consumer Protection Law and city and state weights and measures statutes. It also licenses various types of businesses and activities. The Department also conducts research about consumer issues, educates the public about consumer issues and resolves consumer complaints.

NEW YORK CITY

NEW YORK CITY DEPARTMENT OF CONSUMER AFFAIRS
42 Broadway
New York, New York 10004
(212) 487- 4444

NASSAU COUNTY

The NASSAU COUNTY OFFICE OF CONSUMER AFFAIRS
160 Old Country Road
Mineola, New York 11501
(516) 571 - 2600

SUFFOLK COUNTY

SUFFOLK COUNTY EXECUTIVE OFFICE OF CONSUMER AFFAIRS
P.O. Box 6100
Hauppauge, New York 11788-0099
(631) 853-4600   (8:30 a.m. - 4:00 p.m.)

OFFICE OF THE SHERIFF:

New York: 253 Broadway - New York, N.Y. 10007
                 (212) 240-6715

Bronx: 322 East 149 Street - Bronx, N.Y. 10452
                 (718) 585-1551

Kings: 210 Joralemon Street - Brooklyn, N.Y. 11201
                 (718) 802 - 3545

Queens: 42-71 65 Place - Woodside, N.Y. 11377
                 (718) 803-3091

Richmond: 350 St. Marks Pl.-Staten Island, N.Y. 10301
                 (718) 815-8407

Nassau County: County Office Building - 240 Old Country
                 Road, Mineola, New York 11501
                 (516) 571 - 2113

Suffolk County: 112 Old Country Road, Westhampton New
                 York 11977
                 (631) 852 - 8000

NEW YORK CITY MARSHALS

A copy of a list of city marshals is available at the Small Claims Office, or consult the telephone book for information.

POLICE DEPARTMENT
One Police Plaza
New York, New York 10038
(212) 374-5000

If you are involved in an auto accident and need a copy of the accident report you must contact the local police precinct where the accident occurred **within 30 days.**

After 30 days, contact the New York State Department of Motor Vehicles, (518) 474-0710 obtain an accident report.

ATTORNEY GENERAL'S OFFICE
120 Broadway
New York, New York 10271
(212) 416-8000

Banking Department

The Banking Department regulates all activities relating to the New York State chartered banking industry. The department also enforces laws and policies dealing with consumer credit and other financial services, the prevention of illegal lending, and other consumer abuses.

Education Department

The Education Department licenses approximately 30 professions, including the following:

Physicians and physicians' assistants
Physical therapists
Dentists and dental hygienists
Optometrists
Chiropractors
Veterinarians
Pharmacists
Accountants
Interior designers
Nurses
Podiatrists
Engineers and architects
Acupuncturists
Social workers
Psychologists

Judicial Branch - Appellate Divisions

The Appellate Divisions conduct proceedings to admit, suspend, or disbar attorneys who wish to practice or who are practicing in the courts of New York State.

Insurance Department

The Insurance Department issues licenses and permits, conducts examinations, and administers fines relating to insurance companies, agents, brokers, and adjusters.

Department of Labor

The Department of Labor has regulatory jurisdiction in the areas of employee safety and health, employee earnings, and employee coverage under unemployment insurance.

Department of Motor Vehicles

The Department of Motor Vehicles regulates the registration and titling of motor vehicles and issues drivers' licenses. It also licenses or registers inspection stations, driving schools and instructors, repair shops, dealers and transporters, the vehicle salvage industry, snowmobiles, all-terrain vehicles, motorboats, and unique motor vehicles.

Public Service Commission

The Public Service Commission has the power of general supervision of all gas, electric, water-works corporations, telephone and telegraph lines. Rates for privately owned gas, electric, steam, telephone, telegraph, radio-telephone, and waterworks corporations need Commission approval.

Department of Transportation

The Department of Transportation regulates railroads, buses and trucking companies. It also grants licenses to public utility companies for real estate rights on Department of Transportation-controlled property.

PART IV - COURTHOUSE LOCATIONS

NEW YORK CITY LOCATIONS

New York City Small Claims Court is part of the Civil Court of the City of New York. **Court sessions begin promptly at 6:30 p.m.** You should arrive 30 minutes earlier due to security checks. If you are a senior citizen (65 years of age or older) or you are disabled, or if you work during the evening the Small Claims Clerk will schedule your case during a daytime session.

New York County Civil Court
111 Centre Street
New York, New York 10013
(212) 374 - 5779

Bronx County Civil Court
851 Grand Concourse
Bronx, New York 10451
(718) 590 - 2693

Kings County Civil Court
141 Livingston Street
Brooklyn, New York 11201
(718) 643 - 7914

Queens County Civil Court
89-17 Sutphin Boulevard
Jamaica, New York 11435
(718) 262 - 7123

Richmond County Civil Court
927 Castleton Avenue
Staten Island, New York 10310
(718) 390 - 5421

Midtown Community Court
314 West 54 Street
New York, New York 10019
(212) 374 - 5779

Harlem Community Court
170 East 121 Street
New York, New York 10035
(212) 828-7314

Offices of the **County Clerk** can be located in the New York City
telephone book - white pages (blue section).

NASSAU COUNTY

Small Claims cases are tried in three District Court locations. Small
Claims cases are not, however, heard everyday in every court. You may
telephone the courts listed below to find out their schedule.

Daytime Small Claims Parts   (9:30 a.m.)

Hempstead Part -- 2nd District -- Civil Clerks Office
99 Main Street, Hempstead, New York 11550
Telephone (516) 572-2262

Great Neck Part – 3rd District
435 Middle Neck Road, Great Neck, New York 11023
Telephone: (516) 571-8400

Hicksville Part – 4th District
87 Bethpage Road, Hicksville, New York 11801
Telephone: (516) 571-7090

If you wish to have your case heard in the daytime, you may file your
claim in one of the three courts listed above. There is no limitation with
respect to the selection of the court. Many plaintiffs choose to file in a court
which is convenient to their home.

Night Small Claims (Nassau County)

Civil Part – 1st District
99 Main Street, Hempstead, New York 11550
Telephone: (516) 572-2262

You may initiate a night small claim at the Great Neck Part, Hicksville Part or the 1st District Part during normal business hours. **The evening session is only conducted at 99 Main Street, Hempstead, New York at 6:00 p.m.**

City Court - Long Beach
1 West Chester Street
Long Beach, New York 11561
Telephone: (516) 431 - 1000

Glen Cove
13 Glen Street- Rm. 1R
Glen Cove, New York 11542
(516) 676-0109

To obtain the correct or "legal" name of a business contact:

Nassau County Clerk
County Office Building
Rm. 107 (9:00 am - 4:30 pm)
240 Old Country Road
Mineola, New York 11501
(516) 571-2660

SUFFOLK COUNTY

Suffolk County District Courts are located at the following locations:

First District Court (Civil)
3105 Veterans Memorial Highway
Ronkonkoma, New York 11779
(631) 854-9676

Second District:
375 Commack Road
Deer Park, New York 11729
(631) 854-1950

Third District:
1850 New York Avenue
Huntington Station, New York 11746
(631) 854-4545

32

Fourth District:
North County Complex
Building C-158
Veterans Memorial Highway
Hauppauge, New York 11788
(631) 853-5408

Fifth District:
3105 Veterans
Memorial Highway
Ronkonkoma, New York 11779
(631) 854-9673

Sixth District
150 West Main Street
Patchogue, New York 11772
(631) 854-1440

NIGHT COURT IS HELD IN RONKONKOMA ON WEDNESDAYS AT 6:00 PM.

To obtain the correct or "legal" name of a business contact:

Suffolk County Clerk
310 Center Drive
Riverhead, New York 11901
(631) 852-2000

Appendix 4

A GUIDE
TO
SMALL CLAIMS COURT

New York State
Unified Court System

Judith S. Kaye
Chief Judge

Jonathan Lippman
Chief Administrative Judge

(Effective September, 1996)

TABLE OF CONTENTS

WHAT IS THE SMALL CLAIMS COURT?

The Small Claims Court is an informal court where individuals can sue for money only, up to $3,000, without a lawyer.

For example, if you feel that a person or business damaged something you own, you may sue that person or business for the monetary amount of your damages. You also may sue a person or business for money damages arising out of false advertising or other deceptive practices. You cannot, however, sue in Small Claims Court to compel that person or business to fix the damaged item or to require the performance of the act promised in an advertisement; your lawsuit can be only for money.

Most Small Claims Courts have a clerk who can assist you with the procedures for bringing your lawsuit. In those Town or Village Courts that do not have clerks, the judge may assist you. When this booklet mentions the clerk, and the court you are using does not have a clerk, you should seek the assistance of the judge.

WHO CAN USE THE SMALL CLAIMS COURT?

Anyone over 18 years of age can bring an action in Small Claims Court. If you are younger than 18, your parent or guardian may file the claim for you. Corporations, partnerships, associations, or assignees cannot sue in Small Claims Court,[1] but they can be sued.

If you sue in Small Claims Court, you are the claimant (plaintiff); if you have been sued, you are the defendant. You can sue more than one defendant in the same case if necessary.

If you are sued, and you believe that a third party is responsible for the claim, you may be able to bring that party into the lawsuit as a defendant. Contact the clerk of the Small Claims Court for information about a "third-party action."

A corporation may authorize an attorney, officer, director, or employee of the corporation to appear to defend a claim.

If you choose, you may be represented by an attorney at your own expense, but it is not necessary to have an attorney since Small Claims Court is meant to be a "people's court" where claims may be tried speedily, informally, and inexpensively. The defendant has the same choice. If there are attorneys on both sides, the case may be transferred to a regular part of the court.

---

[1] A partnership may bring a lawsuit in Small Claims Court in the District Courts of Nassau and Suffolk Counties only.

1

WHERE ARE THE SMALL CLAIMS COURTS LOCATED?

There is at least one Small Claims Court in each of the 62 counties in New York State, including at least one in each of the five boroughs of New York City. In the City of New York, the Small Claims Court is part of the Civil Court of the City of New York. In Nassau and Suffolk Counties, the District Courts have Small Claims Parts. All city courts have a Small Claims Part. Town and Village Courts, with the exception of those located in Nassau County, handle Small Claims in the municipalities where they are located. Consult your telephone book for the address and phone number of your local court and call that local court for information.

HOW DO I START A SMALL CLAIMS CASE?

You, or someone on your behalf, must come to the Small Claims Court to file a statement of your claim.

You should be prepared to give a brief statement of the facts that form the basis of your claim. Check any documents relating to your case for the relevant dates and names. If you are suing on a contract or for property damage, you may claim interest as well as damages. You must sue in a court having a Small Claims Part in an area where the defendant lives or works or has a place of business.

You will be required to pay a filing fee of $10.00 if your claim is for $1,000 or less and a filing fee of $15.00 if your claim is for more than $1,000.

When the claim is filed, the clerk will tell you when the case will be tried. The clerk will then send the notice of claim to the defendant by both certified mail and ordinary first class mail. The notice of claim tells the defendant when the case will be tried and gives a brief statement of your claim and the amount of money you are seeking. If the copy of the claim sent by ordinary mail is not returned as undeliverable within 21 days, the defendant is presumed to have received notice even if the claim sent by certified mail has not been delivered.

If the notice is not delivered by the post office, the court will set a new trial date and tell you how to arrange for personal service of the notice of claim on the defendant. Personal service may be made by any person (including a friend or a relative) who is 18 years of age or older, except that you or any other party to the action may not serve the notice of claim.

If service of the notice cannot be made upon the defendant within four months of the date when the action was first started, the action will be dismissed without prejudice to your bringing the action at a later time.

A Small Claims case will not proceed to trial until the defendant has been served with a notice of claim.

MUST I KNOW THE DEFENDANT'S CORRECT NAME?

When filing a Small Claims case, the claimant must provide the name and address of the person or business being sued. If you do not know the correct legal name of the defendant, you can sue using any name under which the defendant does business. However, you should go to the office of the County Clerk in the county where the business is located to find out who owns the business and the legal name of the business. The County Clerk's office keeps a record of the names under which businesses are operated.

If you discover the defendant's correct "legal" name before the trial date, return to the Small Claims Court and have the case papers changed to state the correct name of the defendant.

WHAT IS A COUNTERCLAIM?

Sometimes the defendant may have a claim against the claimant and may countersue the claimant in the same case. This is known as a "counterclaim" and it can be made for up to $3,000 in money damages. The defendant must come to court prepared to prove the counterclaim. You have the right to reply to a counterclaim but are not required to do so.

The defendant is required to file his or her counterclaim with the court within five days of receiving your notice of claim and must pay the court a fee of $3.00 plus the cost of mailing the counterclaim to you. If the defendant fails to file a counterclaim within the five-day period, the defendant may still file the counterclaim until the time of the hearing. The judge then may either proceed with the hearing or adjourn the hearing for a short period of time. However, if the defendant did not file the counterclaim within the five-day period, the judge must adjourn the hearing to a later date if you so request.

If you receive notice of a counterclaim against you, contact the Small Claims Court to see what procedures you should follow. Be prepared to try both your own case and the counterclaim at the time of your hearing.

Any claim or counterclaim for more than $3,000 may not be brought to a Small Claims Court; it must be brought in another part of the court or in another court.

ADJOURNMENTS

Adjournments in Small Claims Court are discouraged. Only the judge can decide if an adjournment is to be granted.

If you are going to ask for an adjournment, you should notify the other party in advance. Either you or someone else on your behalf should appear in court to

3

explain to the judge why you cannot be ready for trial. Some courts permit adjournments to be requested by mail or by telephone (adjournments by telephone are not available in New York City or Nassau and Suffolk Counties), and you should contact the court to find out the method of adjournment. If you do not have a good excuse, your request may be denied and, if you are not ready to go to trial, your case may be dismissed, or, if you are the defendant, an award may be made without your having been heard.

WHAT SHOULD I DO AT TRIAL?

On the date set for trial, you should arrive at the court before the calendar of cases is called. Contact the Small Claims Court to find out the hour at which court begins. If the claimant is late, the case may be dismissed. If the defendant is late, a default judgment against the defendant may be granted.

When you arrive, check the Small Claims calendar posted on the wall outside the courtroom, or with the clerk if there is no calendar posted, to see that your case is scheduled.

When the clerk calls your case, stand and state your name and tell the court that you are ready to proceed with your case. If you are requesting an adjournment, tell the clerk at that time.

The trial is a simple, informal hearing before a judge or arbitrator.

SHOULD I CHOOSE A JUDGE OR AN ARBITRATOR?

In Town and Village Courts and in many other courts, only judges are available to try cases. However, in New York City, Nassau and Westchester counties, the cities of Buffalo and Rochester, and some other locations, both judges and arbitrators are available to try cases.

An arbitrator is an experienced lawyer who serves without pay. Where arbitrators are used, there usually are many arbitrators available and only one or two judges. Your case can be tried by an arbitrator if both sides agree. If you and the defendant agree to have your case heard by an arbitrator, the case probably will be heard sooner because there are more arbitrators than judges.

Do not hesitate to have your case tried by an arbitrator. He or she will apply the same law to your case as the judge would apply. The hearing before an arbitrator is less formal, and you may not be as nervous as you might be before a judge. When an arbitrator determines a case, the decision is final and there is no further appeal by either the claimant or defendant.

4

CAN I CHOOSE TO GO TO MEDIATION?

Yes. There are community dispute resolution centers, under contract to the courts, available in every county in the state. There is normally no charge or a small filing fee. Your case will be scheduled quickly at a time and place convenient to all parties. Matters are confidential and the process is voluntary. Mediation gives you ample time to present your position. You take responsibility to work together on possible solutions with the help of a professionally trained mediator. A written binding agreement can be drawn up by both parties. You can locate your nearest dispute resolution center by checking your telephone book or by obtaining at Small Claims Court the brochure on your local dispute resolution center.

ARE THERE ANY JURY TRIALS?

The claimant in a Small Claims action cannot demand a jury trial. A defendant, however, may demand a trial by jury. If a defendant demands a jury trial, the defendant must pay a jury fee and file a $50.00 "undertaking" (security) with the court to guarantee the payment of costs that may be awarded against the defendant. The defendant also is required to make an affidavit specifying the issues of fact which the defendant desires to have tried by a jury, and stating that such trial is desired and demanded in good faith. The Small Claims clerk will answer your questions regarding the procedures for obtaining a jury trial. Jury trials are held before panels of six jurors.

PREPARING FOR TRIAL

1. *Evidence*

Before trial, you should gather all the evidence necessary to prove your claim or your defense. Anything that will help prove the facts in dispute should be brought to court. This includes photographs, written agreements, an itemized bill or invoice that is receipted or marked "paid," written estimates of the cost of the service or repairs, a receipt for the purchase of an item or the payment of a debt, canceled checks, and correspondence. If you rely on estimates, two different written itemized estimates of the cost of the service or repairs are required. If possible, merchandise that is in dispute should be brought to court.

Testimony, including your own, is evidence. Any witness whose testimony is important to your case may testify. This can be a person who witnessed your transaction or someone whose special knowledge and experience makes him or her an expert on the cost of the service or repairs that were provided or may be required.

You may have to pay an expert witness for his or her time.

2. *Subpoenas*

If you are unable to get a witness to appear voluntarily, you may apply for issuance of a subpoena to the clerk of the Small Claims Court, who will give you the necessary information.

A subpoena is a legal document that commands the person named in the subpoena to appear in court. An expert witness may not be compelled to testify by subpoena, but you may pay the expert witness for coming to court to testify.

You also may apply to the clerk of the Small Claims Court for a "*subpoena duces tecum,*" which is a legal document that directs someone to produce a bill, receipt, or other written document or record you need.

Either party may apply for a subpoena up to 48 hours before the trial date.

You must arrange for service of the subpoena and the payment of a $15.00 witness fee and, where appropriate, travel expenses for the person subpoenaed. Except where the travel is entirely within a city, a subpoenaed witness is entitled to 23 cents a mile as travel expense to and from the court from the place he or she was served with the subpoena. Service of the subpoena may be done by any person (including a friend or relative) who is 18 years of age or older, except that you or any other party to the action may not serve the subpoena.

HOW IS A TRIAL CONDUCTED?

The claimant's case is presented first. After being sworn as a witness, the claimant will tell his or her version of the incident. All papers or other evidence should be shown at this time. When the claimant has finished testifying, the judge or arbitrator or the defendant may ask some questions to clarify matters. Other witnesses can be presented in support of the claimant, and they, too, can be questioned by the judge or arbitrator or the defendant.

The defendant then will be sworn and tell his or her side of the story and present evidence. The defendant also may present other witnesses. The claimant or the judge or arbitrator may ask questions of the defendant and the witnesses called by the defendant.

If you are suing a business, be certain to ask the defendant's witness the full and correct legal name of the business and the name of the person who owns the business. If the name of the business is different from the name you wrote in your notice of claim, ask the judge or arbitrator to make any correction in the name on your notice of claim.

6

After all the evidence is in, the judge or arbitrator will consider the evidence and render a decision. The decision will be mailed to the parties within a few days of the hearing. In rare cases, the decision may be announced immediately after the trial.

DISCLOSURE OF ASSETS

It is your responsibility to collect information on the defendant's assets in the event you receive a judgment in your favor and the defendant does not pay you. [See "How Can I Collect My Judgment?"] The court has the power, before entering a judgment, to examine the defendant, to order the defendant to disclose his or her assets, and to restrain the defendant from disposing of those assets.

WHAT HAPPENS IF ONE PARTY DOES NOT APPEAR?

If the claimant does not appear in court when the calendar is called, the case will be dismissed.

If the defendant does not appear, the court will direct an "inquest" (hearing). That means that the claimant will go before the judge or arbitrator to present evidence to prove his or her case without the defendant presenting any evidence. If the claimant's case is proved, a "default" judgment will be awarded against the defendant.

If a default judgment is granted because the defendant did not appear, or the case is dismissed because the claimant did not appear, the losing party may ask the court to re-open the case and restore it for a trial upon a showing of good cause. Contact the clerk for the procedure used to re-open the case. The clerk also will set a date when both sides are to return to court.

On the return date, the judge will decide whether to re-open the case. However, both sides should be prepared for trial in the event the case is re-opened.

SETTLEMENTS

In a lawsuit, one of the parties must always lose. Although you believe you are entitled to win, the judge or arbitrator may rule against you. Therefore, parties to a Small Claims action are encouraged to settle their cases whenever possible. You should seriously consider a reasonable offer of settlement.

If the case is settled before the day of trial and the money has been paid, notify the clerk by mail. You do not have to appear in court.

If a case is settled but the money has not been paid, or if settlement talks are not completed, the claimant may wish to appear in court so that the case is not

7

dismissed and ask the judge for "adjournment pending settlement." A new date then will be set for trial. If the settlement does not work out, both parties should appear in court on the new adjourned date prepared for trial.

CAN I APPEAL THE CASE IF I LOSE?

If your case was tried by a judge, you may appeal the decision if you believe justice was not done. You cannot appeal if your case was tried by an arbitrator.

Technical mistakes made during the trial are not grounds for reversal. The appellate court will consider only whether substantial justice was done.

Very few Small Claims cases are appealed. The expense of appealing is rarely justified in a Small Claims action. Taking an appeal may require retaining an attorney. In addition, the party who is appealing must purchase a typed transcript of the trial proceedings from the court reporter, or from the court when audio recording of the trial is authorized. If no stenographic minutes were taken, the party appealing will be required to prepare a statement of what took place during the proceeding or, in some courts, the judge or clerk will write this statement. If a statement is used, the party who is not appealing will have the opportunity to offer changes to the statement.

If you decide to appeal, you must file a notice of appeal and pay the required fee within 30 days after the judgment is entered. Consult the Small Claims clerk if you wish further information about starting an appeal.

The party appealing the judgment can temporarily prevent its enforcement pending the decision on the appeal. To do this, a bond or undertaking must be filed with the court to guarantee payment of the judgment should the party lose the appeal. If you receive a notice of appeal, you should call the court to find out if an undertaking has been posted: if not, you may take steps necessary to collect the judgment immediately, or you may wait until the appeal has been decided.

WHAT DO I DO IF I WIN?

If the claimant wins, the court will enter a judgment for a sum of money. The court also may require the claimant to take certain action -- for example, return damaged merchandise to the defendant -- before entering judgment.

HOW CAN I COLLECT MY JUDGMENT?

Winning a judgment does not guarantee you will collect.

The court provides some help in collection of judgments. For example, prior to rendering judgment, the court can order the defendant to disclose his or her assets and restrain the defendant from disposing of them. However, you must take the necessary steps to obtain payment of your judgment.

After winning a judgment in your favor, you should try to contact the losing party to collect your judgment. If the defendant does not pay you, you may need the services of an enforcement officer -- a sheriff, city marshal, or a constable. You must provide this officer with the information needed to locate assets (money or property) of the defendant, and the enforcement officer then can seize those assets to satisfy your judgment. The enforcement officer may request mileage and other fees before he or she seizes the assets. In many circumstances, these fees later can be added to the original judgment amount you receive from the defendant.

Property that may be reached by an enforcement officer includes bank accounts, wages, houses or other real estate, automobiles, stocks, and bonds.

LOCATING ASSETS

1. *Information Subpoenas*

If a Small Claims judgment has been entered in your favor, you may obtain an information subpoena or subpoena from the Small Claims clerk upon payment of a $2.00 fee. If you request it, the clerk will assist you in the preparation and use of the information subpoena forms. Some stationery stores also sell information subpoena forms.

An information subpoena is a legal document that may help you to discover the location of assets of the judgment debtor (defendant). It is a legal direction to a person or institution to answer certain questions about where the assets of the defendant are located. The information subpoena may be served upon the judgment debtor and upon any person or corporation that you believe has knowledge of the judgment debtor's assets -- for example, the telephone company, landlord, or bank. Separate forms are used for service on the judgment debtor and service on any other person or corporation.

The person or corporation served with an information subpoena must answer the questions served with the subpoena within seven days of receipt.

The information subpoena, accompanied by two copies of a set of written questions and a prepaid addressed return envelope, may be served by ordinary or by certified mail, return receipt requested.

2. *Bank Accounts and Wages*

One simple way to improve the chances of collecting your judgment is to learn the name and address of the bank where the defendant keeps a savings or checking account. A way to do this is to look at the back of a canceled check you or a friend may have given to the defendant. With this information, the enforcement officer can seize money in the defendant's account and use the funds to satisfy your judgment.

Another way is to find out the name and address of the defendant's employer. If you sued an employed person, you may be able to collect your judgment out of his or her salary. To do this, the enforcement officer can serve an "income execution" on the judgment debtor. This execution requires the debtor to pay 10% of the judgment debtor's salary to you until the judgment is paid, provided the debtor's gross earnings are above a certain minimum amount set by federal law (currently $142.50 per week).

3. *Real Property*

If the defendant owns real property, you may be able to collect your judgment from its sale. The clerk will direct you to the proper office where you can check property ownership. You will have to obtain a transcript of your Small Claims judgment from the court and file it with the County Clerk. You then should consult the sheriff, who may conduct a sale at public auction. It is your responsibility to prepare the papers to sell the property. The sheriff, after deducting his or her fees and expenses, and, after paying off any prior mortgage, tax liens, and judgments, will send the balance to you, up to the amount of your judgment, plus interest.

4. *Personal Property*

Your judgment can be paid from the sale of defendant's personal property, such as automobiles. Contact the enforcement officer for details of the expenses and fees required. It is your responsibility to prepare the papers required to sell the property.

If you give an enforcement officer the model, year, and license plate number as well as the location of the defendant's automobile, the officer can seize it, sell it at auction, and pay your judgment with the proceeds. You can check with the New York State Department of Motor Vehicles to learn whether the defendant owns an automobile (fill out form MV-15). You can also find out from the Department of Motor Vehicles whether a bank or finance company already has a claim against the defendant's car.

If the defendant has a large unpaid auto loan, a bank or finance company might be entitled to payment of the loan from the sale of the defendant's vehicle before your judgment can be satisfied.

OTHER ENFORCEMENT PROCEDURES

1. *Claims Based on Motor Vehicle Ownership*

If your claim was based on the defendant's ownership or operation of a motor vehicle, you may be able to have the Department of Motor Vehicles suspend the defendant's driver's license and auto registration until the judgment is paid. To take advantage of this procedure, you must have a judgment for over $1,000 that has remained unpaid for more than 15 days after it becomes final. Ask the clerk for details of this procedure.

2. *Licensing Agencies*

If the judgment debtor is engaged in a business that is licensed or certified, you may notify the appropriate state or local authority if the judgment remains unpaid 35 days after the judgment debtor receives notice of entry of the judgment. The failure to pay a judgment may be considered by the licensing authority as a basis for the revoking, suspending, or refusing to grant or renew a license to operate a business. At the end of this guide is a list of prominent licensing or certifying authorities and a description of the types of businesses each oversees. If the Small Claim arises out of the conduct of the defendant's business, the court will determine the appropriate licensing or certifying authority for the defendant in your case.

If the judgement debtor is a business that the court finds to be engaged in fraudulent or illegal conduct, you have the right to notify the Attorney General and, if the business is licensed, the appropriate licensing authority as well.

3. *Prior Unsatisfied Judgments*

If a defendant has failed to pay three or more judgments despite having sufficient resources to pay them, you may be able to sue the defendant for triple damages. Check with the clerk to see if your defendant is listed in the index of unsatisfied judgments maintained by the court.

PROMINENT STATE LICENSING OR CERTIFYING AUTHORITIES

1. *Department of Agriculture and Markets*

The Department's regulatory authority includes licensing of and the issuing of permits for:
- Manufacturers, wholesalers, and handlers of frozen desserts;
- Persons acting as dealers, brokers, or commission merchants for the sale of farm products;
- Milk dealers;

- Food processing establishments;
- Refrigerated warehouses, locker plants, and fresh foods;
- Operators of purebred dog kennels;
- Anyone who deals in, handles, or transports domestic animals, or operates a livestock auction.

2. *Division of Alcoholic Beverage Control*

The Division issues licenses and permits authorized by the Alcohol Beverage Control Law for the manufacture, distribution, and sale of alcoholic beverages within the State.

3. *Banking Department*

The Department regulates all activities relating to the New York State-chartered banking industry. The Department also enforces laws and policies dealing with consumer credit and other financial services, the prevention of illegal lending, and other consumer abuses.

4. *Commission on Cable Television*

The Commission issues confirmation certificates for new franchises, renewals of franchises, and loss of services from a franchise.

5. *Education Department*

The Department licenses approximately 30 professions, including the following:
- Physicians and physicians' assistants;
- Physical therapists;
- Chiropractors;
- Dentists and dental hygienists;
- Veterinarians;
- Pharmacists;
- Nurses;
- Podiatrists;
- Optometrists;
- Engineers and architects;
- Accountants;
- Psychologists;
- Social workers;
- Acupuncturists;
- Interior designers.

The Department also licenses private schools, business schools, and agents for private schools. It registers private schools for handicapped children and all post-secondary educational programs, including professional schools.

6. *Judicial Branch - Appellate Divisions*

The Appellate Divisions conduct proceedings to admit, suspend, or disbar attorneys who wish to practice or who are practicing in the courts of New York State.

7. *Department of Environmental Conservation*

The Department's principal regulatory programs include: water pollution control; air pollution; radioactive waste control; solid and hazardous waste management; waste transport; mining; public water supply; dams; and protection of freshwater and tidal wetlands, streams, and navigable waters.

8. *Insurance Department*

The Department issues licenses and permits, conducts examinations, and administers fines relating to insurance companies, agents, brokers, and adjusters, including the following:
- Any firm, association, or corporation doing insurance business in the State;
- Anyone acting as a life, accident, or health insurance agent;
- Anyone acting as an insurance broker;
- Anyone acting as an insurance adjuster.

9. *Department of Labor*

The Department has regulatory jurisdiction in the areas of employee safety and health, employee earnings, and employee coverage under unemployment insurance.

10. *Division of the Lottery*

The Division has the statutory responsibility to conduct lottery games for the benefit of education and is empowered to license ticket sellers.

11. *Department of Motor Vehicles*

The Department regulates the registration and titling of motor vehicles and issues drivers' licenses. It also licenses or registers inspection stations, driving schools and instructors, repair shops, dealers and transporters, the vehicle salvage industry, snowmobiles, all-terrain vehicles, motorboats, and unique motor vehicles.

12. *Department of Public Service*

The Public Service Commission has the power of general supervision of all gas, electric, water-works corporations, and telephone and telegraph lines. Rates for privately owned gas, electric, steam, telephone, telegraph, radio-telephone, and waterworks corporations need Commission approval.

13. *Racing and Wagering Board*

The Board issues licenses to the following concerning thoroughbred, harness, and quarterhorse racing:
- Owners;
- Trainers;
- Assistant trainers;
- Jockeys;
- Drivers;
- Jockeys' agents;
- Veterinarians;
- Farriers;
- Race track employees.

It also issues licenses required to conduct a race meeting with pari-mutuel wagering, issues licenses to suppliers and renters of bingo equipment, and games-of-chance equipment, and issues identification numbers for those conducting games-of-chance or bingo operations.

14. *Department of Social Services*

The Department regulates residential foster care of children, family day care facilities, day care centers for children of eligible guardians, and adult residential care. Special care homes for unwed mothers, victims of domestic violence, and workshops for the blind are also regulated by the Department.

15. *Department of Taxation and Finance*

The Department is responsible for the registration of:
- Alcoholic beverage distributors;
- Motor fuel distributors;
- Diesel motor fuel retailers and bulk purchasers;
- Owners of diesel motor vehicles;
- Flea market promoters;
- Vendors required to collect sales tax;
- Organizations exempt from sales tax.

The Department is responsible for the licensing of:
- Wholesale dealers of cigarettes;
- State lottery ticket vendors.

The Department issues permits for motor vehicles subject to highway-use or fuel-use taxes. It also appoints cigarette tax agents.

16. *Department of Transportation*

The Department regulates railroads and bus and trucking companies. It also grants licenses to public utility companies for real estate rights on Department of Transportation-controlled property.

PROMINENT LOCAL LICENSING OR CERTIFYING AUTHORITIES

If you desire a list of the most prominent local licensing or certifying authorities, you should contact the court clerk for this information.

FORM 1

CIVIL COURT OF THE CITY OF NEW YORK
SMALL CLAIMS PART
STATEMENT OF CLAIM

INSTRUCTIONS:
Place only ONE letter or number in each space and leave a blank space between words.

I CLAIMANT'S INFORMATION

(Your)

LAST NAME

FIRST NAME

MIDDLE INITIAL

ADDRESS

BOROUGH, CITY, TOWN OR VILL.   STATE   ZIP

OTHER INFO
(Doing Business As or In Care Of)

PHONE NO. (   )

II DEFENDANT'S INFORMATION*

(Their)

LAST NAME
(or Business Name)

FIRST NAME

MIDDLE INITIAL

ADDRESS

BOROUGH, CITY, TOWN OR VILL.   STATE N Y   ZIP

OTHER INFO
(Doing Business As or In Care Of)

PHONE NO. (   )

III CLAIM

Amount Claimed: $ _____ (Maximum $3,000)   Date of Occurrence or Transaction: _____

Place of occurrence, if Auto Accident _____

PRIMARY REASON FOR CLAIM (Check One):

Damage caused to:
- ☐ automobile
- ☐ other personal property
- ☐ real property
- ☐ person

Failure to provide:
- ☐ proper repairs
- ☐ proper services
- ☐ proper merchandise
- ☐ goods paid for

Failure to return:
- ☐ security
- ☐ property
- ☐ deposit
- ☐ money loaned

Failure to pay:
- ☐ salary
- ☐ for services rendered
- ☐ insurance claim
- ☐ rent
- ☐ commissions
- ☐ for goods sold and delivered

Breach of:
- ☐ contract
- ☐ lease
- ☐ warranty
- ☐ agreement

Loss of:
- ☐ luggage
- ☐ property
- ☐ time from work
- ☐ use of property

Returned:
- ☐ check (bounced)
- ☐ check (stopped)

Other: (Be brief) _____

IDENTIFYING NUMBER(S) - (Receipt #, Claim #, Account #, Policy #, Ticket #, License #, Plate #'(s) _____

Today's Date _____   Signature of Claimant or Agent _____

*DEFENDANT'S NAME: The legal name will be required in order to obtain an enforceable judgment. If the Defendant is a business, its full and correct business name should be obtained from the Office of the County Clerk in the county in which the business is located.
DEFENDANT'S ADDRESS: You must indicate the proper street address of the Defendant. A Post Office Box is not acceptable.
NOTE: If the Claim is as a result of an automobile accident, the Claim must be OWNER against OWNER.

CIV-SC-50 (Revised 1/96)

CERT'D #

COA CODE

CLAIM AMT.

FEE
STANDARD FEE PLUS POSTAGE
- ☐ CLAIMANT V. DEFENDANT
- ☐ DEFENDANT V. THIRD PARTY

NO FEE; POSTAGE ONLY
- ☐ CLAIMANT V. ADD'L DEFENDANT
- ☐ WAGE CLAIM TO $300

LANGUAGE _____

DATE DATA ENTERED _____

DATE NOTICES MAILED _____

CASE TYPE:
- MULTI DFT ☐   CTR/CLM ☐
- 3 PARTY ☐   CRS/CMPLT ☐

FIRST DATE _____

DAY COURT
- ☐ STATUTORY   ☐ OTHER

FORM 2
Side 1

CIVIL COURT OF THE CITY OF NEW YORK
COMMERCIAL CLAIMS PART
STATEMENT OF CLAIM

INSTRUCTIONS:
Place only ONE letter or number in each space
and leave a blank space between words.

(Your)

I. CLAIMANT'S INFORMATION

BUSINESS NAME

OTHER INFO
(Doing Business As
or In Care Of)

PRINCIPAL
OFFICE ADDRESS

BOROUGH, CITY,
TOWN OR VILL.

STATE [N Y]   ZIP

PHONE NO. (   )

(Their)

II. DEFENDANT'S INFORMATION

LAST NAME
or business name

FIRST NAME   MIDDLE INITIAL

ADDRESS
(of Residence or Place of
Business or Employment)

BOROUGH, CITY,
TOWN OR VILL.

STATE [N Y]   ZIP

OTHER INFO
(Doing Business As
or In Care Of)

PHONE NO. (   )

III. CLAIM

Amount Claimed: $ _____ (Maximum $3,000)   Date of Occurrence or Transaction: _____

Briefly state your claim here: (Include Indentifying Number(s) — Receipt #, Claim #, Account #, Policy #, Ticket #, License #).

_____

_____

_____

_____

_____

_____

Today's Date _____   Signature of Claimant or Agent _____

YOU MUST COMPLETE ONE OF THE CERTIFICATIONS ON THE REVERSE SIDE

CIV-SC-70 (Revised 1/93)

(FOR OFFICE USE ONLY)

CERT'D #

COA CODE

CLAIM AMT.
$

FEE
STANDARD FEE PLUS POSTAGE
☐ CLAIMANT V. DEFENDANT
NO FEE; POSTAGE ONLY
☐ DEFENDANT V. THIRD PARTY
☐ CLAIMANT V. ADD'L DEFENDANT
☐ WAGE CLAIM TO $300

LANGUAGE

DATE DATA ENTERED

DATE NOTICES MAILED

CASE TYPE:
MULTI DFT ☐   CTR/CLM ☐
3 PARTY ☐   CRS/CMPLT ☐

FIRST DATE

DAY COURT
☐ STATUTORY   ☐ OTHER
☐ CONSUMER TRANSACTION
☐ OTHER COMMERCIAL CLAIMS

FORM 2
Side 2

COMPLETE THIS SECTION FOR A COMMERCIAL CLAIM

*CERTIFICATION: (NYCCCA 1803-A)

I hereby certify that no more than five (5) actions or proceedings (including the instant action or proceeding) pursuant to the commercial claims procedure have been initiated in the courts of this State during the present calendar month.

_____
Signature of Claimant

_____
Signature of Notary / Clerk / Judge

*NOTE: The Commercial Claims Part will dismiss any case where this certification is not made.

**COMPLETE THIS SECTION FOR A COMMERCIAL CLAIM
ARISING OUT OF A CONSUMER TRANSACTION**

†CERTIFICATION: (NYCCCA 1803-A)

I hereby certify that I have mailed a demand letter by ordinary first class mail to the party complained against, no less than ten (10) days and no more than one hundred eighty (180) days before I commenced this claim.

I hereby certify, based upon information and belief, that no more than five (5) actions or proceedings (including the instant action or proceeding) pursuant to the commercial claims procedure have been initiated in the courts of this State during the present calendar month.

_____
Signature of Claimant

_____
Signature of Notary / Clerk / Judge

†NOTE: The Commercial Claims Part will not allow your action to proceed if this certification is not made and properly completed.

CIV-SC-70 (Reverse 11/90)

FORM 3

**State of New York
Department of State** } ss:

I hereby certify, that a diligent examination has been made of the index of corporation certificates filed by this department for a Certificate of Incorporation for _____ and that upon such examination, no such Certificate or Incorporation has been found on file in this Department.

***

Witness my hand and the official seal of the Department of State at the City of Albany, this 06th day of January two thousand.

Special Deputy Secretary of State

FORM 4

CERTIFICATE OF INCORPORATION

OF

_____

Under Section 402 of the Business Corporation Law

      The undersigned, a natural person over the age of eighteen years, desiring to form a corporation pursuant to the provisions of the Business Corporation Law of the State of New York, hereby certifies as follows:

      FIRST: The name of the corporation is

_____

hereinafter sometimes called "the corporation."

      SECOND: The purpose for which the corporation is formed is as follows:

          To engage in any lawful act or activity for which corporations may be organized under the Business Corporation Law, provided that the corporation is not formed to engage in any act or activity that requires the consent or approval of any state official, department, board, agency or other body, without such consent or approval first being obtained.

      For the accomplishment of the foregoing purposes, and in furtherance thereof, the corporation shall have and may exercise all of the powers conferred by the Business Corporation Law upon corporations formed thereunder, subject to any limitations contained in Article 2 of said law or the provisions of any other statute of the State of New York.

      THIRD: The office of the corporation in the State of New York is to be located in the County of New York.

      FOURTH: The aggregate number of shares that the corporation shall have the authority to issue is 150 Shares of Common Stock, with no par value.

FORM 5

Civil Court of the City of New York

County of _____

Part _____ Date _____

Index Number _____

Hon. _____

Plaintiff(s)/Petitioner(s),

against

Defendant(s)/Respondent(s)

STIPULATION OF SETTLEMENT

The parties understand that each party has the right to a trial, the right to see a Judge at any time and the right not to enter into a stipulation of settlement. However, after a review of all the issues, the parties agree that they do not want to go to trial and instead agree to the following stipulation in settlement of the issues in this matter:

_____

_____

_____

_____

_____

_____

_____

_____

_____

_____

_____

_____

_____

_____

_____

_____

_____

_____

_____

_____

_____

_____

CIV-LT-30 (Revised. September, 1997)

Page _____ of _____

FORM 6

DEMAND LETTER

_____

_____

_____

Date: _____

To: _____
    Name of Defendant

    _____

    _____
    Address

    You have not paid a debt owed to _____ , which you in-curred on _____ , 20 __ . The amount remaining unpaid on the debt is $ _____ . Demand is hereby made that this money be paid. Unless payment of this amount is received by the undersigned no later than _____ , 20__ , a lawsuit will be brought against you in the Commercial Claims Part of the Court.

    If a lawsuit is brought, you will be notified of the hearing date, and you will be entitled to appear at the hearing and present any defense you may have to this claim.

    (If applicable) Our records show that you have made the following payment in partial satisfaction of this debt (Fill in dates and amounts paid) _____ .

    A copy of the original debt instrument -- your agreement to pay -- is attached. [The names and addresses of the parties to that original debt agreement are _____

_____

_____

(to be completed if claimant was not a party to the original transaction)].

_____

_____

                                         Typed or Printed Name and Address
                                                 of Claimant

DC 106 M-3108 10/00

FORM 7

SUPREME COURT OF THE STATE OF NEW YORK -- COUNTY OF NEW YORK

--x

                      Plaintiff,

               Index No. _____ / _____

    - against -

               AFFDAVIT OF
               SELF-REPRESENTED PERSON
          Defendant.   **IN SUPPORT OF APPLICATION**
               FOR ADJOURNMENT

--x

_____, being duly sworn, deposes and says:

(1) I am [*cross out one*] the plaintiff / defendant in this case. A motion for _____ (Motion Sequence No.

_____) is currently pending. I seek an adjournment of the return date thereof until _____ for the following reason:

_____ .

(2) I have not obtained consent to this request from all adversaries. On _____, I personally, by the following means

[*specify:*] _____ attempted to contact _____, attorney for _____, and to seek consent . Such

consent was not obtained because [*cross out the inapplicable phrase:*]

        (i) it was refused by _____ .

        (ii) it was not possible to reach said attorney (or an associate with authority).

As part of this communication, a message was transmitted advising said attorney that an appearance would be made in the Motion

Support Office Courtroom (Room 130) today at 9:30 AM for the purpose of making an application for the requested adjournment.

        (3) Wherefore, I respectfully request an adjournment until _____ .

Dated: _____
    New York, New York

                               _____ (Signature)

                               _____ (Print Name)

                               _____ (Address)

                               _____ (Phone)

NOTE: THIS DOCUMENT MUST BE SERVED ON ADVERSARIES AS PROVIDED IN THE CIVIL PRACTICE LAW AND
RULES.

FORM 8

Civil Court Of The City Of New York

Small Claims /Commercial Claims Part
County of Queens
89-17 Sutphin Boulevard
Jamaica, N.Y. 11435

Today's Date: WJM

Index No.:

The Hearing of your claim has been set for 6:30 P.M. in the
Small Claims /Commercial Claims Part Courtroom
First Floor, Room 101
**Only the Judge presiding at the Hearing can grant an adjournment.
The Clerk cannot grant any change in the scheduled date or time.**

INSTRUCTIONS TO CLAIMANT

HEARING

You must be present, with any witness(es) and/or other proof of your claim, at the time and place indicated above.

If your claim is for property damage, in order to prove your claim you must produce, at the time of trial, either:

(1) An Expert Witness (for example, a Mechanic)
(2) A Paid Receipt (itemized, marked "Paid," and signed), or
(3) Two Estimates for services or repairs (itemized and signed)

Once service of the Notice of Claim is complete, you may request the Clerk to issue a Subpoena for Records and/or a Subpoena to Testify, to compel someone to appear. Such Subpoenas are issued by the Court without any fee, but you will be required to pay a fee to the person on whom the Subpoena is served. Your request for such Subpoena must be made of the Clerk before the date of the Hearing.

If you have not received a copy of the booklet "A Guide to Small Claims" or "A Guide to Commercial Claims", please request one.

JUDGES AND ARBITRATORS

The Judge can only hear a limited number of cases at each session of Court. Most Hearings are held before volunteer Arbitrators who are attorneys with at least five years of experience and thoroughly knowledgable in the law.

The decision of a Judge is subject to appeal but no appeal of an Arbitrator's decision is permitted since there is no official court transcript of Hearings held before Arbitrators.

Either party may choose to have the case heard **only** by the Judge, by responding **"by the Court,"** at the time of the calendar call. If you request your case "by the Court" it is quite possible that you will have to return for trial at another time.

INSTRUCTIONS FOR ANSWERING THE CALENDAR CALL

If you are ready for trial and you are willing to have your case heard by an Arbitrator . . . . **Answer: (Your Name/Claimant), Ready**
If you wish: to request a postponement of your case,
to change the amount of the claim, or
to add an additional party . . . . **Answer: Your Name, Application**
If you are ready for trial but you are not willing to have your case heard by
an Arbitrator and you are requesting that the case be heard **only** by the Judge . . . . **Answer: Your Name, Ready By the Court**

RESULT OF NON-APPEARANCE (DEFAULT)

If the Defendant (the person you are suing) fails to answer or appear for trial an Inquest may be held. In an Inquest, you (the Claimant) must prove your case to the satisfaction of the Arbitrator even though the Defendant is not present. In almost all instances the Inquest will result in a **Judgment** in favor of the Claimant.

If you (the Claimant who is suing) fail to appear, the case will generally be **Dismissed.**

SETTLEMENT

If you and the Defendant are able to work out a settlement, the written agreement (Stipulation of Settlement) should be filed with the Court. This should be done on or before the date set for the Hearing. The document provided to the Court must include the SC Number of your case and the year.

If the Defendant admits the claim but desires more time to pay, and you are not willing to accept the plan for payment, you must both appear personally on the date set for the Hearing. At that time, with the aid of the Court, you may be able to reach agreement on the terms of payment.

AVISO: ESTA INFORMACIÓN ESTÁ DISPONIBLE EN ESPAÑOL BAJO PEDIDO.
— BRING THIS SHEET WITH YOU AT ALL TIMES —

CIV-SC-67   (Revised 9/97)

FORM 9

Side 1

Civil Court of the City of New York Index No. S.C. _____

COUNTY OF _____

Small Claims/Commercial Claims Part _____

Claimant(s),

against

NOTICE OF JUDGMENT

Defendant(s),

DECISION: After Trial/Inquest, the decision in the above action is as follows:

A. ☐ Judgment and Award in favor of_____

B. ☐ Judgment in favor of Defendant, dismissing claim. No monetary award.

Award amount ....$ _____

Interest ....$ _____

Disbursements ....$ _____

TOTAL JUDGMENT ....$ _____

(Information below and on the reverse side applies to all parties when an award has been granted.)

(Information below and on the other side is not applicable.)

Date: _____   By: _____
  J.C.C./Arbitrator

INFORMATION FOR THE JUDGMENT DEBTOR
(the party against whom a money judgement has been entered)

YOU HAVE A LEGAL OBLIGATION TO PAY THIS JUDGMENT.
YOU MUST PRESENT PROOF TO THE COURT UPON SATISFACTION OF THE JUDGMENT.

Your failure to pay the judgment may subject you to any one or any combination of the following:

a) garnishment of wage(s) and/or bank account(s);

b) lien, seizure and/or sale of real property and/or personal property, including automobile(s);

c) suspension of motor vehicle registration, and/or drivers license, if the underlying claim is based on judgment debtor's ownership or operation of a motor vehicle;

d) revocation, suspension, or denial of renewal of any applicable business license or permit;

e) investigation and prosecution by the State Attorney General for fradulent or illegal business practices;

f) a penalty equal to three times the amount of the unsatisfied judgment plus attorney's fees if there are unpaid claims.

If you did not appear in court on the day the Hearing was held, you are a defaulting party. A judgment may have been taken against you even though you were not in court. If that is so, you may apply to the court in writing and ask to have the default judgment opened. You must give the judge a reasonable excuse for your failure to appear in court and show that you have a meritorious defense. The Judge may open your default judgment and give you another chance to go to court.

("Information for the Judgment Creditor" is on the reverse side.)

THE JUDGMENT IS VALID FOR A PERIOD OF 20 YEARS. IF THE JUDGMENT IS NOT COLLECTED UPON THE FIRST ATTEMPT, FURTHER ATTEMPTS TO COLLECT MAY BE MADE AT A LATER DATE.

CIV-SC-92 (Revised 5/92)

FORM 9
Side 2

INFORMATION FOR THE JUDGMENT CREDITOR
(the party in whose favor a money judgment award has been entered)

1. Contact the judgment debtor (the party who owes you money) either directly or through that party's attorney if the party was represented by an attorney, and request payment. You have a right to payment within 30 days. Upon satisfying the judgment, in accordance with CCA §1811(c), the judgment debtor shall present appropriate proof to the court.

2. a) If the judgment debtor fails to pay **within 30 days**, contact (by phone or in person) either a New York City Marshal or the Sheriff in the county where the judgment debtor *has property*. If you do not know where the judgment debtor has property, then contact a New York City Marshal or the Sheriff in the county where the judgment debtor *resides*.

   b) Be prepared to provide the City Marshal or the Sheriff with the following information:
      1) The SC# of your case, including the year, which appears at the top on the reverse side.
      2) The county in which the case was tried.
      3) Your name, address and telephone number.
      4) The name and address of the judgment debtor.
      5) The name and address of the judgment debtor's employer and the location of the judgment debtor's real property and/or personal property, including automobile(s). *Information regarding employment or assets of the judgment debtor can be obtained through the use of an Information Subpoena. See 3b).*

   c) Fees paid by you, the judgment creditor, to the City Marshal or to the Sheriff in an attempt to collect the judgment will be added to the total judgment.

3. A judgment creditor is also entitled:
   a) to the issuance by the Clerk of a Restraining Notice. Proper service of the Restraining Notice will prohibit the receiving party from transferring any assets or interest belonging to the judgment debtor until the Sheriff or Marshal executes (collects) on the judgment.

   b) to the issuance by the Clerk, upon request and at nominal cost, of Information Subpoenas where a judgment remains unsatisfied.

   c) to place a lien against the judgment debtor's real property.

4. In addition to any other rights, a judgment creditor may also be entitled:
   a) to recover an unpaid judgment through garnishment of wage(s) and/or bank account(s) and/or the sale of the judgment debtor's real property and/or personal property;

   b) to notify the Department of Motor Vehicles of the unsatisfied judgment as a basis for the suspension of the judgment debtor's motor vehicle registration and/or driver's license if the underlying claim is based on the debtor's ownership or operation of a motor vehicle;

   c) to notify the appropriate state or local licensing authority of an unsatisfied judgment as a basis for possible revocation, suspension, or denial of renewal of a business license;

   d) to notify the State Attorney General if the judgment debtor is a business and appears to be engaged in fraudulent or illegal business practices; and;

   e) to begin an action against the judgment debtor for a penalty equal to three times the amount of the unsatisfied judgment and attorney's fees where the judgment debtor is a business and there are two or more unsatisfied small claims judgments against that judgment debtor.

To contact a City Marshal:
Look in the Yellow Pages under City Marshal.

To contact a County Sheriff:

County	Address	Borough	Zip Code	Phone Number
Bronx	880 River Avenue,	Bronx, N.Y.	10452	(718) 293-3900
Kings	Municipal Building,	Brooklyn, N.Y.	11201	(718) 802-3545
New York	253 Broadway,	New York, N.Y.	10007	(212) 240-6715
Queens	County Court House,	L.I. City, N.Y.	11101	(718) 392-4950
Richmond	350 St. Mark's Place,	Staten Island, N.Y.	10301	(718) 447-0041

("Information for the Judgment Debtor" is on the reverse side.)

CIV-SC-92 Reverse (Revised 9/92)

FORM 10

Civil Court of the City of New York   **APPLICATION FOR A PRO SE SUMMONS**

PARTIES

PLAINTIFF: (YOUR name and complete address, including your apartment number and telephone number.)
[NOTE: If the claim is based on an auto accident, the claim must be *Owner* against *Owner*].

_____

_____

_____

DEFENDANT(S): (The full legal name and street address (no box number) of the party(ies) you are suing.
Indicate whether you are suing this party as a person or a business.)
[NOTE: If you are suing a business, indicate whether it is a partnership, a corporation or an individual with a business
certificate. This information can be obtained in the County Clerk's Office in the county in which the business
exists. Failure to check this information may result in a judgment which cannot be executed.]

_____

_____

_____

CLAIM

REASON FOR CLAIM:

Damage caused to:	☐ automobile	☐ person	☐ property other than automobile
Failure to provide:	☐ repairs	☐ proper services	☐ goods ordered
Failure to return:	☐ security	☐ property	☐ deposit ☐ money
Failure to pay for:	☐ wages ☐ rent	☐ services rendered ☐ commissions	☐ insurance claim ☐ money loaned ☐ goods sold and delivered
Breach of:	☐ contract	☐ lease	
Loss of:	☐ luggage	☐ property	☐ time from work ☐ use of property
Returned:	☐ check (bounced)	☐ merchandise (not reimbursed)	

Other: (Be brief)

_____

_____

DETAILS OF CLAIM:

Amount of Claim: (Limit $25,000 for each Cause of Action) $_____

Date of Occurence: _____

Place of Occurence: _____

If Car Accident: YOUR license plate #_____ DEFENDANT'S license plate #_____

Identifying Number(s): _____
(Receipt #, Claim #, Account #, Policy #, Ticket #, etc.)

_____   X _____
Today's Date   Signature of Plaintiff

CIV-GP-59 (Revised 11/92)

FORM 11

SMALL CLAIMS COMPLAINT FORM

PLAINTIFF'S NAME (please print)_____

(if a partnership name each individual partner)

(If plaintiff is doing business under a trade name, print trade name below)

_____

PLAINTIFF'S ADDRESS _____

_____

NAME OF PERSON OR FIRM YOU ARE SUING (please print) _____

_____

STREET ADDRESS (must be within Nassau County) _

_____

CAUSE OF ACTION (state amount, dates and details)_____

_____

_____

_____

_____

_____

_____

WITH INTEREST FROM _____

_____

    The undersigned acknowledges that ___ he has been informed prior to the commencement of this action, that ___ he shall be deemed to have waived all right to appeal except on the sole ground that substantial justice has not been done.

    The undersigned has also been advised that supporting witnesses, account books, receipts and other documents required to establish the claim herein must be produced at the hearing.

_____
Plaintiff

DC89cM-433
Revised 3/98

FORM 12

DC 94 M-2056   Revised 3/98

COMMERCIAL CLAIMS COMPLAINT FORM

[ ] Commercial Transaction

[ ] Consumer Transaction

CLAIMANT'S NAME (please print) _____

Address _____

Telephone _____

NAME OF PERSON OR FIRM YOU ARE SUING (please print) _____

_____

Street Address (must be within Nassau County)_____

_____

CAUSE OF ACTION (state amount, dates and details)_____

_____

_____

_____

_____

_____

_____

_____

With Interest From _____

CERTIFICATION (Sec. 1803-A & 1809-A UDCA)

I, _____ (name) am a/an _____

_____ (officer, director or employee) of _____

_____ (claimant-corporation, partnership or association) and have been authorized to represent the claimant in this commercial claim action, which has its principal office in the State of New York. I certify to the truthfulness of the within claim and that no more than five (5) such actions or proceedings (including the instant action or proceeding) have been initiated during the present calendar month. I further certify that I have the requisite authority to bind the corporation, partnership or association in a settlement or trial of any claim or counterclaim.

The undersigned acknowledges that he/she has been informed prior to the commencement of this action, that he/she shall be deemed to have waived all right to appeal except on the sole ground that substantial justice has not been done.

The undersigned has also been advised that supporting witnesses, account books, receipts and other documents required to establish the claim herein must be produced at the hearing.

Date: _____   _____

                                      Signature

_____

Clerk or Notary

FORM 13

3.14.01   25

SUFFOLK COUNTY DISTRICT COURT COMPLAINT FORM

COURT DATE April 25 2001
TIME & DIST. 2:00 pm

INDEX NO.
DATE MAILED 3/16/01

For official use only

☐ SMALL CLAIMS (DAY)   ☐ SMALL CLAIMS (NIGHT)   ☑ COMMERCIAL CLAIM   ☐ CONSUMER TRANSACTION

PLAINTIFF'S NAME ADDRESS AND ZIP CODE If plaintiff is a business you must use your true business name	DEFENDANT'S NAME. ADDRESS AND ZIP CODE If defendant is a business you must use the defendant's true business name
Corp	
PRINT (Last Name) (First Name)	PRINT (Last Name) (First Name)
BAYSHORE, N.Y. 11706	HAUPPAUGE, NY 11788
(City) (State) (Zip Code)	(City) (State) (Zip Code)
Tel. No. 631 -	Tel. No.
PRINT (Last Name) (First Name)	PRINT (Last Name) (First Name)
(City) (State) (Zip Code)	(City) (State) (Zip Code)
Tel. No.	Tel. No.

CAUSE OF ACTION (CHECK ONE)

- ☐ (5)   PERSONAL INJURIES
- ☑ (10) PROPERTY DAMAGE
- ☐ (15) LOSS OF PERSONAL PROPERTY
- ☐ (20) GOODS SOLD AND DELIVERED
- ☐ (25) BREACH OF CONTRACT OR WARRANTY
- ☐ (35) WORK. LABOR AND SERVICES

- ☑ (40) MONIES DUE
- ☐ (50) PAYMENT OF LOAN
- ☐ (70) REFUND ON DEFECTIVE MERCHANDISE
- ☐ (80) REFUND ON DEFENDANT'S DEFECTIVE WORK. LABOR AND/OR SERVICES
- ☐ (85) ACTION AS SHOWN ON COMPLAINT FORM

STATE AMOUNT. DATES AND DETAILS:

Co Cancelled Service, has not Returned locker Set - PAID invoices #3412 and #34345 on 8/12/00 - Remaining balance due for May Service for 143.95 and 450.00 For Locker Set.

TOTAL AMOUNT $ 593.45

The undersigned acknowledges that he/she has been advised that supporting witnesses, account books, receipts and other documents required to establish the claim herein must be produced at the hearing. The undersigned further certifies to the best of his/her knowledge, the defendant is not in the military service.

CERTIFICATION FOR COMMERCIAL CLAIMS ONLY (UDCA 1803-A)

The undersigned hereby certifies that no more than five (5) actions or proceedings (including the instant action) pursuant to the commercial claims procedure have been initiated in the courts of this state during the present calendar month.

DATED: 3/14/01

Corp

PLAINTIFF)

Notary Public, State of New York
Qualified in Suffolk County
Commission Expires May 27, 2___

CLERK/NOTARY

(AS AUTHORIZED AGENT OF PLAINTIFF)

(AS PARENT AND NATURAL GUARDIAN)

PLEASE NOTE: THIS FORM MUST BE SIGNED BEFORE A COURT CLERK OR NOTARY

FORM 14

Side 1

DISTRICT COURT, COUNTY OF SUFFOLK
SECOND DISTRICT HELD AT BABYLON
===
COMMERCIAL CLAIMS SUMMONS

INDEX #:

Take notice that:

has asked judgment in this Court against you for $593.45 upon the
following claim:

MONIES DUE

There will be a hearing before the court upon this claim on
April 25, 2001 at 2:00p o'clock at the SECOND District Court, located at
375 COMMACK ROAD, DEER PARK, NY 11729

You must appear and present your defense and any counterclaim you may
desire to assert at the hearing at the time and place set forth above (a
corporation must be represented by an attorney or any authorized officer,
director or employee). IF YOU DO NOT APPEAR, JUDGMENT WILL BE ENTERED
AGAINST YOU BY DEFAULT EVEN THOUGH YOU MAY HAVE A VALID DEFENSE. If your
defense or counterclaim, if any, is supported by witnesses, account books,
receipts or other documents, you must produce them at the hearing. The
Clerk, if requested, will issue subpoenas for witnesses, without fee
thereof.

If you intend to file a COUNTERCLAIM against the plaintiff, you should
file a statement containing the facts of the counterclaim with the Clerk
of the Court, along with the filing fee of $3.00 plus $.34 for each named
plaintiff, within five (5) days of receiving this notice. NOTE: If you do
not choose this method of filing a counterclaim, you may request
permission from the judge at the hearing.

If you admit the claim, but desire time to pay, you must appear
personally on the day set forth for the hearing, and state to the Court
your reasons for desiring time to pay.

March 15, 2001

Clerk of the Court

NOTE: If you desire a jury trial, you must, before the day upon which you
have been notified to appear, file with the Clerk of the Court a written
demand for a trial by jury. You must also pay to the clerk a jury fee of
$55.00 and file an undertaking in the sum of $50.00 or deposit such sum,
in cash, to secure the payment of any costs that may be awarded against
you. You will also be required to make an affidavit specifying the issues
of fact which you desire to have tried by a jury and stating that such
trial is demanded in good faith.
Under the law, the court may award $25.00 additional costs to the
plaintiff if a jury trial is demanded by you and a decision is rendered
against you.

FORM 14
Side 2

ADJOURNMENTS

Requests for adjournments must be made in writing to the court with notice of the request given to all parties. Requests may also be made in person on the court date. No requests for adjournments will be accepted by phone. All requests for adjournments are submitted to the judge/arbitrator on the court date for approval. The court does not notify the parties of the new court date if the adjournment request is granted. You must contact the court to ascertain the new date.

PROOF OF CLAIM; DEFENSES TO CLAIM

On the court date you must submit all items necessary to prove the claim or to defend against the claim. Contracts, agreements, receipts, canceled checks, photographs and other documents should be produced at trial. Property damage may be proven by two itemized written estimates or by one itemized paid bill. Persons having actual knowledge of the facts and circumstances of the claim, or who are experts in a field may be present to testify. Expert witnesses cannot be subpoenaed to testify since most require compensation to appear in court.

DUTY TO PAY JUDGMENTS

(A) Any person, partnership, firm or corporation which is sued in a small/commercial claims court for any cause of action arising out of its business activities, shall pay any judgment rendered against it in its true name or in any name in which it conducts business. "True name" includes the legal name of a natural person and the name under which a partnership, firm or corporation is licensed, registered, incorporated or otherwise authorized to do business. "Conducting business" as used in this section shall include, but not limited to , maintaining signs at business premises or on business vehicles; advertising; entering into contracts; and printing or using sales slips, checks, invoices or receipts. Whenever a judgment has been rendered against a person, partnership, firm or corporation in other than its true name and the judgment has remained unpaid for thirty-five days after receipt by the judgment debtor of notice of its entry, the aggrieved judgment creditor shall be entitled to commence an action in small/commercial claims court against such judgment debtor, notwithstanding the jurisdictional limit of the court, for the sum of the original judgment, costs, reasonable attorney's fees, and one hundred dollars.

(B) Whenever a judgment which relates to activities for which a license is required has been rendered against a business which is licensed by a state or local licensing authority and which remains unpaid for thirty-five days after receipt by the judgment debtor of notice of its entry and the judgment has not been stayed or appealed, the state or local licensing authority shall consider such failure to pay, if deliberate or part of a pattern of similar conduct indicating recklessness, as a basis for the revocation, suspension, conditioning or refusal to grant or renew such license. Nothing herein shall be construed to preempt an authority's existing policy if it is more restrictive.

FORM 15

CITY COURT OF WHITE PLAINS
77 SOUTH LEXINGTON AVE.
WHITE PLAINS, N.Y. 10601
(914) 422-6050

APPLICATION FORM

Payment by mail must be Certified Check or Money Order only, (Payable to White Plains Court)

Check One: _____ Small Claims (Amt. $1,000 or less filing fee $10.00) ___

(Amt. exceeding $1,000 filing fee $15.00)

_____ Commercial Claim (Filing fee -$20.00 plus postage $4.28 =$24.28)

_____ Counter Claim (Filing fee $3.00 plus postage .34= $3.34)

Consumer Transaction: _____ Yes _____ No

Plaintiff Info: **Defendant Info:**

_____   _____
Name   Name

_____   _____
Name   Name

_____   _____
Address   Address

_____   _____
City, State & Zip Code   City, State & Zip Code

_____   _____
Telephone No.   Telephone No.

Amt. Claim is for: $_____   **(DO NOT ADD FILING FEE)**

Briefly state reason for claim: _____

_____

_____

* If claim submitted via mail   _____
  Signature must be Notarized.   Signature of Claimant

COMPLETE THIS SECTION FOR COMMERCIAL CLAIMS ONLY

I certify that no more than five (5) actions or proceedings (including the instant action or Proceeding) pursuant to the commercial claims procedure have been initiated in the courts of this state during the present calendar month.

_____   _____
Signature of Notary, Clerk, Judge   Signature of Claimant

COMPLETE THIS SECTION FOR CONSUMER TRANSACTIONS ONLY

I hereby certify that I have sent a demand letter to _____
defendant, at least 10 days, but no more than 180 days, before commencing this action.

Dated: _____   _____
                                                            Signature of Claimant

FORM 16

STATE OF NEW YORK: COUNTY OF WESTCHESTER
WHITE PLAINS CITY COURT
77 SOUTH LEXINGTON AVENUE
WHITE PLAINS, NEW YORK 10601

SMALL CLAIMS SUMMONS
TEL - 914-422-6050
INDEX: CC- ——————

DEFENDANT:

——————— INC.

NEW ROCHELLE, N.Y. 10801

PLAINTIFF:

——————————— INC.

LONG ISLAND CITY, NY 11101

TAKE NOTICE the above plaintiff(s) seeks judgment in this Court against you for $545.51 together with costs, upon the following claim:

LEASED EQUIPMENT & PERFORMED SERVICES, BREACH OF CONTRACT.

THERE WILL BE A HEARING before this Court upon this claim on May 5, 1999 at 07:00 PM in the Small Claims Part B, held at the above address.

YOU MUST APPEAR and present your defense and any Counterclaim you may desire to assert at the Hearing at the time and place set forth above (a corporation must be represented by an attorney or any authorized officer, director or employee). IF YOU DO NOT APPEAR, JUDGMENT WILL BE ENTERED AGAINST YOU BY DEFAULT, EVEN THOUGH YOU MAY HAVE A VALID DEFENSE. If your defense or Counterclaim, if any, is supported by witnesses, account books, receipts, or other documents, you must produce them at the Hearing. The Clerk, if requested, will issue subpoenas for witnesses, without fee. IF YOU ADMIT THE CLAIM, BUT DESIRE TIME TO PAY, YOU MUST APPEAR PERSONALLY ON THE DAY SET FOR THE HEARING.

DATED: December 4, 1998   _Patricia _____, Clerk
IF YOU DESIRE A JURY TRIAL, you must befoCHIEF CLERK, WHITE PLAINS CITY COURT been notified to appear,
file with the Clerk of the Court a written demand for a trial by jury. You must also pay to the
Clerk a jury fee of $55.00 and file an undertaking in the sum of $50.00 or deposit such sum in
cash to secure the payment of any costs that may be awarded against you. You will also be
required to make an affidavit specifing the issues of fact you desire to have tried by a jury,
stating that such trial is desired and demanded in good faith. Under the law, the Court may
award $25.00 additional costs to the plaintiff(s) if a jury trial is demanded by you and a
decision is rendered against you.

** NOTE ** THE Court does not encourage adjournments. Only the Judge may grand an adjournment
request. All requests MUST be in writing with notice to the other party and for good cause. If
you do not receive notice of a new date you or someone on your behalf MUST appear in Court to
explain to the Judge why you cannot be ready for trial.

A defendant if he wishes to file a counterclaim shall do so by filing with the clerk a statement
containing such counterclaim within 5 days of receiving the notice of claim. At the time of such
filing the defendant shall pay to the clerk a filing fee of $3.32 which is required
pursuant to this subdivision. The clerk shall forthwith send notice of the counterclaim by
ordinary first class mail to the claimant. If the defendant fails to file the counterclaim in
accordance with the provisions of this subdivision, the defendant retains the right to file
the counterclaim, HOWEVER the counterclaim may, but shall not be required to, request and
obtain an adjournment to a later date. The claimant may reply to the counterclaim,
but shall not be required to do so.

!!!BRING THIS NOTICE WITH YOU AT ALL TIMES!!!
*** A COPY OF THE BOOKLET, "A GUIDE TO SMALL CLAIMS PART",
IS AVAILABLE AT ANY CITY COURT.

FORM 17

CLERK _____

DATE 12/4/98

~~SMALL CLAIM~~ /COMM. CLAIM #

HEARING DATE _____ 5/5/99 _____ PART B AT ~~1:30 P.M.~~/ 7:00 P.M.
AT THE CITY COURT OF WHITE PLAINS 77 SOUTH LEXINGTON AVENUE, W.P., N.Y. 10601

FAILURE TO APPEAR MAY RESULT IN THE DISMISSAL OF YOUR CLAIM (S).

INSTRUCTIONS TO PLAINTIFF--PROOF OF CLAIM

THERE IS A SPECIAL RULE OF LAW WHICH DISPENSES WITH THE NECESSITY OF HAVING AN EXPERT
WITNESS (SEE ITEM D FOR EXCEPTIONS) TESTIFY IN CASES WHERE A PARTY IS SEEKING TO PROVE THE
AMOUNT OF MONEY SPENT FOR REPAIRS AND/OR SERVICES OF ANY KIND WHEN THE REPAIRS AND/OR
SERVICES HAVE BEEN COMPLETED AND THE BILLS ARE FULLY PAID/ SEE ITEM A)

A.   IF YOU HAVE A SIGNED ITEMIZED BILL

     A SIGNED ITEMIZED PAID BILL MUST BE FILED TEN (10) DAYS PRIOR TO THE HEARING WITH
     NOTICE TO THE OTHER SIDE BY CERTIFIED MAIL.

B.   IF YOU HAVE ESTIMATED BILLS

     IF YOU HAVE ONLY ONE (1) ESTIMATED BILL, YOU MUST HAVE YOUR EXPERT WITNESS IN COURT
     TO TESTIFY ON YOUR BEHALF, AT THE HEARING.

C.   IF YOU HAVE TWO (2) ESTIMATED BILLS

     IF YOU HAVE NOT PAID FOR THE REPAIRS OR SERVICES PURSUANT TO YOUR CLAIM. YOU MUST
     SUBMIT TWO (2) ITEMIZED ESTIMATES FROM TWO (2) DIFFERENT EXPERTS AS TO THE
     REASONABLE VALUE FOR THOSE REPAIRS AND/OR SERVICES. IF THIS IS THE CASE YOU WILL
     NOT NEED AN EXPERT WITNESS IN THE COURT TO TESTIFY ON YOUR BEHALF AT THE HEARING.

D.   IF YOU ARE CLAIMING DEFECTIVE WORKMANSHIP AND/OR MATERIALS

     IF YOU ARE CLAIMING DEFECTIVE WORKMANSHIP AND/OR MATERIALS, YOU MUST HAVE YOUR
     EXPERT WITNESS IN THE COURT ON THE HEARING DATE TO TESTIFY ON YOUR BEHALF

AT THE TIME THAT YOU ARE RECEIVING THIS FORM YOU ARE ALSO BEING GIVEN A BOOK THAT MAY
ASSIST YOU IN ANSWERING SOME FURTHER QUESTIONS THAT YOU MAY HAVE REGARDING SMALL CLAIMS.

FORM 18

COUNTY OF   INDEX NO.:

against

Plaintiff(s)

AFFIDAVIT
OF
SERVICE

Defendant(s)

STATE OF NEW YORK, COUNTY OF NEW YORK   ss.:

being duly sworn, deposes and says: that deponent is not a party

to this action, is over 18 years of age and resides in
That on
deponent served the within

on

defendant therein named,

INDIVIDUAL by delivering thereat a true copy of each to said defendant personally: deponent knew said person so served to be the person described as said defendant
therein. (5)He identified (her) himself as such.

CORPORATION , by delivering thereat a true copy of each to
personally; deponent knew said   so served to be the   described as the named
defendant and knew said individual to be the   thereof.

SUITABLE AGE PERSON by delivering thereat a true copy of each to
a person of suitable age and discretion. That person was also asked by deponent whether said premises was the defendant's
and the reply was affirmative.

AFFIXING TO DOOR, ETC. by affixing a true copy of each to the door of said premises, which is defendant's
within the state. Deponent was unable, with due diligence to find defendant or a person of suitable age and discretion thereat, having verified
defendant's   with
and having called there on

MAILING On   deponent also enclosed a copy of same in a postpaid sealed wrapper properly addressed to defendant at defendant's
and deposited said wrapper in a post office of the United States Postal Service within New York State.

DESCRIPTION Deponent describes the individual served to the best of deponent's ability at the time and circumstances of service as follows:

Sex	Skin Color	Hair Color	Age (Approx.)	Height (Approx.)	Weight (Approx.)

USE IN NYC CIVIL CT. Other identifying features:

The language required by NYCRR 2900.2(e), (f) & (h) was set forth on the face of said summons(es).

MILITARY SERVICE I asked the person spoken to whether defendant was in active military service of the United States or of the State of New York in any capacity whatever
and received a negative reply.
The source of my information and the grounds of my belief are the conversations and observations above narrated.
Upon information and belief I aver that the defendant is not in the military service of New York State or of the United States as that term is defined
in either the State or Federal statutes.

SWORN TO BEFORE ME ON

LICENSE NO.

FORM 19

Civil Court of the City of New York

[PLEASE PRESS HARD]

COUNTY OF _____

Part _____

Index No. _____

_____

Claimant(s) / Plaintiff(s),

against

Defendant(s),

**AFFIDAVIT IN SUPPORT OF
ORDER TO SHOW CAUSE**
To Vacate a Judgment and
to Restore to the Calendar

Address:

State of New York, County of _____ ss.:

_____, being duly sworn, deposes and says:
(Print Your Name)

Defendant's Initials

**1.
PARTY**
_____ a) I am the party named as defendant in the above entitled action.

**2.
SERVICE**
_____ a) I have been served with a summons and complaint in this action [NOTE: If Small Claims skip #3, go to #4.]
_____ b) I have not been served, and my first notice of legal action was [NOTE: if you complete any of #2b, skip #3, #4 & #5, go to #6.]
_____ a notice of Default Judgment mailed to me.
_____ a Restraining Notice on my bank account.
_____ a copy of an Income Execution served on _____.
_____ Other: _____

**3.
APPEAR-
ANCE**
_____ a) I did not appear and answer in the Clerk's Office because: [NOTE: If you complete #3a, skip to #6.]
_____

b) I did appear and answer in the Clerk's Office
_____ and I received a date for trial.
_____ but the answer was entered late.
_____ Other: _____

**4.
TRIAL**
On the Date of Trial before Judge/Arbitrator _____
_____ a stipulation (a written agreement) was made between claimant/plaintiff and defendant.
_____ a judgment was entered after the trial.
_____ a judgment was entered against me by default for my failure to appear.
_____ Other: _____

**5.
EXCUSE**
My reason for not
_____ complying with the stipulation which was made is _____
_____ following the order of the Court is _____
_____ appearing in court on the date scheduled for trial is _____
_____ Other: _____

**6.
DEFENSE**
I allege that I have a good defense because: _____
_____

**7.
PRIOR
ORDER**
_____ a) I have not had a previous Order to Show Cause regarding this index number.
_____ b) I have had a previous Order to Show Cause regarding this index number but I am making this further application because: _____

**8.
REQUEST**
_____ I request that the Judgment be vacated, that the case be restored to the calendar, and permission to serve these papers in person.

Sworn to before me this _____ day of _____, 19_____

_____
(Signature of Defendant)

_____
(Signature of Court Employee and Title)

CIV-GP-17 (Revised 8/90)

FORM 20

Civil Court of the City of New York

COUNTY OF _____

_____ Part

Index No. _____

_____

_____
                                   Claimant(s) / Plaintiff(s),

against

_____

_____
                                   Defendant(s),

ORDER TO SHOW CAUSE

TO VACATE DEFAULT JUDGMENT AND

TO RESTORE TO THE CALENDAR

Upon the annexed affidavit of _____
                                              (Defendant)

sworn to on ____4/9/____ , and upon all the papers and proceedings herein:
                 (Date)

LET the Claimant(s) / Plaintiff(s) or Claimant(s) / Plaintiff(s) attorney(s) show cause at:

The Civil Court of the City of New York
(Small Claims Part) (Commercial Claims Part) (Special Term, Part I)

Located at: _111 Centre St rm 353_

County of: _ny_

on: _April 30, 2001_ at _6:30_ AM/PM,

or as soon thereafter as counsel may be heard, why an Order should not be made:

VACATING the Judgment, restoring the case to the calendar, and/or granting such other and further relief as may be just.

PENDING the hearing of this Order to Show Cause and the entry of an Order thereon, let all proceedings on the part of the Claimant(s) / Plaintiff(s), Claimant(s) / Plaintiff(s) attorney(s) and agent(s) and any Marshal or Sheriff of the City of New York for the enforcement of said Judgment be stayed.

SERVICE of a copy of this Order to Show Cause, and annexed Affidavit, upon the:

Claimant(s) / Plaintiff(s) or named attorney(s):   Sheriff or Marshal:
(Judge to Initial)   (Judge to Initial)

___ by Personal Service by "In Hand Delivery"   ___ by Personal Service by "In Hand Delivery"
___ by Certified Mail, R. R. R.   OR   ___ by Certified Mail, R. R. R.
___ by First Class Mail with official   ___ by First Class Mail with official
_____ Post Office Certificate of Mailing   _____ Post Office Certificate of Mailing
on or before _4-16-01_ ,   shall be deemed good and sufficient.

PROOF OF SUCH SERVICE may be filed in the Clerk's office before the return date of this Order to Show Cause, or with the Clerk in the Part indicated above on the return date of this Order to Show Cause.

Attorney(s):   Sheriff / Marshal: **MAIL TO:**

_____   NYC Sheriff   Marion A. Burstock # 7
_____   253 Broadway   36-35 ___ Boulevard
_NY NY 10023_   NYP NY 10007   PO Box 610700
                                      ___ side NY 11361 870

___4/9/___
   Date   Judge, Civil Court
CIV-GP-47 (Revised 9/92)   **IN ANTICIPATION OF DELAYS**   **JUDGE ROLANDO T. ACOSTA**
                 DUE TO THE METAL DETECTORS, IT IS
                 SUGGESTED YOU ARRIVE AT LEAST

FORM 21
Side 1

813584

Civil Court of the City of New York

County of _____
Part

Index Number _____

Claimant(s)/Plaintiff(s)/Petitioner(s)
against

**INFORMATION SUBPOENA
AND
RESTRAINING NOTICE**

_____
(Judgment Debtor)

_____
(Address)

_____
(City, State, Zip Code)

Defendant(s)/Respondent(s)

_____
(Social Security Number)

THE PEOPLE OF THE STATE OF NEW YORK

TO: _____, the person to be examined and/or restrained:

A Judgment was entered in this court on _____, in favor of _____ and

against _____ in the amount of $ _____, together with interest,

costs and disbursements for a total of $ _____, of which $ _____ remains due and unpaid.

INFORMATION SUBPOENA

Because you, the person to whom this subpoena is directed, either reside, are regularly employed or have an office for the regular transaction of business in _____ County of the State of New York, you must answer, in writing under oath, separately and fully, each question in the questionnaire accompanying this subpoena. You must return the answers, together with the original of the questions, within seven (7) days after your receipt of the questions and this subpoena, to _____

at _____

False swearing, or failure to comply with this Subpoena, is punishable as a contempt of court.

RESTRAINING NOTICE

Be advised that in accordance with Section 5222(b) of the Civil Practice Law and Rules **(which is printed in full on the reverse)** you are hereby forbidden to make or permit any sale, assignment or transfer of, or any interference with any property in which you have an interest, except as provided for in that Section. This notice also covers all property which may in the future come into your possession or custody.

Following CPLR §5222(a) a restraining notice is <u>not</u> effective against the employer of a Judgment Debtor where the property sought to be recovered or restrained consists of wages or salary due to the Judgment Debtor.

Disobedience of this Restraining Notice is punishable as a contempt of court.

_____
Date

_____
Chief Clerk, Civil Court

- SEE REVERSE SIDE -

CIV SC 60 (Revised June 2000)

FORM 21
Side 2

CIVIL PRACTICE LAW AND RULES

SECTION 5222(b) Effect of restraint; prohibition of transfer; duration. A judgment debtor or obligor served with a restraining notice is forbidden to make or suffer any sale, assignment, transfer or interference with any property in which he or she has an interest, except upon direction of the sheriff or pursuant to an order of the court, until the judgment or order is satisfied or vacated. A restraining notice served upon a person other than the judgment debtor or obligor is effective only if, at the time of service, he or she owes a debt to the judgment debtor or obligor or he or she is in the possession or custody of property in which he or she knows or has reason to believe the judgment debtor or obligor has an interest, or if the judgment creditor or support collection unit has stated in the notice that a specified debt is owed by the person served to the judgment debtor or obligor or that the judgment debtor or obligor has an interest in specified property in the possession or custody of the person served. All property in which the judgment debtor or obligor is known or believed to have an interest then in and thereafter coming into the possession or custody of such a person, including any specified in the notice, and all debts of such a person, including any specified in the notice, then due and thereafter coming due to the judgment debtor or obligor, shall be subject to the notice. Such a person is forbidden to make or suffer any sale, assignment or transfer of, or any interference with, any such property, or pay over or otherwise dispose of any such debt, to any person other than the sheriff or the support collection unit, except upon direction of the sheriff or pursuant to an order of the court, until the expiration of one year after the notice is served upon him or her, or until the judgment or order is satisfied or vacated, whichever event first occurs. A judgment creditor or support collection unit which has specified personal property or debt in a restraining notice shall be liable to the owner of the property or the person to whom the debt is owed, if other than the judgment debtor or obligor, for any damages sustained by reason of the restraint. If a garnishee served with a restraining notice withholds the payment of money belonging to or owed to the judgment debtor or obligor in an amount equal to twice the amount due on the judgment or order, the restraining notice is not effective as to other property or money.

SECTION 5222(e) Content of Notice....

NOTICE TO JUDGMENT DEBTOR

Money or property belonging to you may have been taken or held in order to satisfy a judgment or order which has been entered against you. Read this carefully.

YOU MAY BE ABLE TO GET YOUR MONEY BACK

State and federal laws prevent certain money or property from being taken to satisfy judgments or orders. Such money or property is said to be "exempt." The following is a partial list of money which may be exempt:

1. Supplemental security income, (SSI);
2. Social security;
3. Public assistance (welfare);
4. Alimony or child support;
5. Unemployment benefits;
6. Disability benefits;
7. Workers compensation benefits;
8. Public or private pensions; and
9. Veterans benefits

If you think that any of your money that has been taken or held is exempt, you must act promptly because the money may be applied to the judgment or order. If you claim that any of your money that has been taken or held is exempt, you may contact the person sending this notice.

Also, YOU MAY CONSULT AN ATTORNEY, INCLUDING LEGAL AID IF YOU QUALIFY. The law (New York Civil Practice Law and Rules, Article 4 and Sections 5239 and 5240) provides a procedure for determination of a claim to an exemption.

CIV-SC-60 Reverse (Rev. 2/95)

FORM 21

Side 3

Civil Court of the City of New York

County of _____
           Part

Index Number _____

Claimant(s)/Plaintiff(s)/Petitioner(s)
against

Defendant(s)/Respondent(s)

QUESTIONS AND ANSWERS
In connection with
INFORMATION SUBPOENA
regarding

_____
(Judgment Debtor)

_____
(Address)

_____
(City, State, Zip Code)

_____
(Social Security Number)

State of New York, County of _____ ss.:

_____, being duly sworn, deposes and says:
              (Name of Deponent)

I am the _____ of _____, and acknowledge receipt of an
           (Title)   (Name of organization)

Information Subpoena naming _____ as Judgment Debtor.

The Answers below are based upon information contained in the records of the recipient.

#1. Q. Please provide the Debtor's full name as indicated on his/her application
    A.

#2. Q. Please set forth the last known home address and telephone number for the Debtor's residence, if different from the address shown above.
    A.

#3. Q. Does the Judgment Debtor have an account with your organization and/or are you currently holding any deposits and/or security? If so, what is the account number, and what is/are the amount(s) on deposit?
    A.

#4. Q. Do your records indicate that the Debtor is employed? If so, please list the name and address of the employer and the salary as indicated in your records.
    A.

#5. Q. Did the Debtor list any bank references on his/her application? If so, set forth the name and address of said bank(s) and account number(s), if available.
    A.

#6. Q. Do your records indicate the location of any other assets of the Debtor? If so, please give the location and description of any other assets.
    A.

The answers given to the above questions are true and complete to the best of my knowledge.

Sworn to before me this _____ day of _____, 20 ___

_____
       Notary Public

_____
Signature (before a Notary Public)

WHEN COMPLETED, RETURN THE ORIGINAL COPY OF THIS FORM TO: _____
                                                        (Judgment Creditor's Name and Address)

<u>DO **NOT**</u> RETURN THIS FORM TO THE CIVIL COURT

CIV-SC-61 (Revised, June, 2000)

FORM 21
Side 4

Civil Court of the City of New York

County of _____

Part

Index Number _____

Claimant(s)/Plaintiff(s)/Petitioner(s)
against

AFFIDAVIT OF SERVICE
of an
INFORMATION SUBPOENA

_____
(Judgment Debtor)

_____
(Address)

_____
(City, State, Zip Code)

Defendant(s)/Respondent(s)

_____
(Social Security Number)

State of New York, County of _____ ss.:

_____, being duly sworn,
(Name of Deponent)

deposes and says:

I am over 18 years of age and not a party to this action. At _____ AM/PM on
(Time)

_____ at _____
(Date)   (Address)

in the County of _____, City of New York, I served an
(Name of County)

Information Subpoena in this matter on:_____,
(Name of Person Served)

known to me to be the Witness named herein by mailing a true copy thereof, by Certified

Mail, Return Receipt Requested.

Sworn to before me this _____ day of _____, 20____

_____
(Signature of Notary Public)

_____
(Signature of Deponent)

CIV-SC-63 (June,2000)

THE CIVIL COURT
of
THE CITY OF NEW YORK

Instructions for Service of an Information Subpoena

RESTRICTIONS:

A Subpoena from the Civil Court of the City of New York may be served only within the City of New York or in Nassau County or Westchester County. Service elsewhere within the State of New York may be done only with the written permission of a Judge

An agency of the city, county or state government, or a public library may be subpoenaed only with the written permission of a Judge.

PROCEDURES:

1) Make a photocopy of the Subpoena and a photocopy of the questions to be answered.

2) Place the **photocopy** of the Subpoena, together with the **original and the photocopy** of the questions to be answered, in an envelope addressed to the person from whom you desire the information. Include a stamped, self-addressed envelope for use by the deponent to return the answered questions to you.

3) Anyone NOT A PARTY TO THE ACTION, who is over the age of 18 and not a Police Officer may "serve" the Subpoena. To "serve" the Subpoena, the person who is serving it should mail the envelope to the witness by Certified Mail, Return Receipt Requested.

4) The person who "served" the Subpoena must fill out the Affidavit of Service on the reverse side of this sheet and have it Notarized.

5) Retain the Affidavit of Service for further procedures if the witness fails to comply with the Subpoena.

CIV-SC-63 Reverse (Revised 3/96)

Winning in the New York Small Claims Courts Order Form

Price: $21.95
Sales Tax: $1.86
Shipping: $3.95
Total Price per book: $27.76

Please visit www.smallclaimsbook.com if you have any questions about the content of the book.

- Order by Phone: 1-800-247-6553 **credit card orders only.**
  Order 24 hours a day, 7 days a week

- Order by Mail: Send this order form to:
  BookMasters, Inc. PO Box 388, Ashland, OH 44805

- Order by FAX: Send this order form to: 1-419-281-6883

- Order on line at: www.atlasbooks.com or send an e-mail to order@bookmasters.com

**Please send me _____ copy (copies) of the book:
Winning in the New York Small Claims Courts**

Ship to:

Name:_____

Address:_____

City:_____ State:_____ Zip:_____

Telephone:_____

e-mail address:_____

Payment:

_____ My money order made payable to BookMasters, Inc. is enclosed.

My Credit Card is: ☐ Visa ☐ MasterCard ☐ Amex ☐ Discover

Card # _____Exp. Date___/___

Name on Card: _____

Signature: _____